MARY BERRY'S
BEST
DESSERTS

MARY BERRY'S
BEST
DESSERTS

DORLING KINDERSLEY
London • New York • Sydney

A DORLING KINDERSLEY BOOK

www.dk.com

First published in Great Britain in 1997
by Dorling Kindersley Limited,
9 Henrietta Street, London WC2E 8PS

10 9 8 7 6 5 4 3 2

Derived from *Mary Berry's Desserts and Confections,* 1991

A CIP catalogue record for this book is available from the British Library
ISBN 0 - 75130 - 485 - 9

Reproduced by Colourscan, Singapore
Printed and bound in Hong Kong by Dai Nippon

FOREWORD

What's for pudding? A question so often in our minds. This is a collection of good-looking, good-tasting recipes that I hope will answer just that question.

Whether you are planning a grand finale to a special meal, seeking new ways to serve old family favourites, choosing for a coffee morning or bridge tea, or wanting to tempt the young with snacks when they come home from school, in this book you will find a wide range of fabulous choices.

Included in my collection are wonderful variations on perennials like Lemon Meringue Pie, Apple Pie and Crêpes Suzette, or if you are interested in mastering the classics like Apple Strudel and Crème Brûlée, you will discover how easy they are to prepare using the recipes in this book. However, if simple dishes are your choice, try a Peach, Raspberry or Kiwi Fruit Fool. If, like me, you delight in hearing 'Mmm!' and 'Ooh!' as you serve dessert, Double Chocolate Mousse Cake and Tiramisù won't disappoint, and I will guarantee that the Meringue Mushrooms will please children from six to ninety-six.

I happen to believe that desserts can be good for you as well as just plain good. They can add heartiness to a light menu and lighten a substantial one. Desserts can supply nutritional foods, such as milk, fruit or grain products, which may be missing from the rest of the day's meals. Even if you, or members of your family, are watching your waistlines, you can enjoy desserts in thinner slices or smaller servings, and still conform to healthy eating guidelines.

Full-colour photographs of every recipe show you what to expect, and step-by-step instructions, many of them illustrated, guide you through each technique in preparation. To make great desserts more glorious, there are dozens of garnishes, decorations and serving tips to help you make every dish as pleasing to the eye as it is to the palate.

A *very* special 'thank you' goes to Jeni Wright, who spent many hours working with me on perfecting the collection. All that remains is for me to wish you 'Bon Appétit', with the hope that this dessert collection gives you as much pleasure to prepare and enjoy, as it did for me to put it together.

CONTENTS

MOUSSES AND SOUFFLÉS

Light, fluffy mousses and soufflés – made from fruit, chocolate, nuts and cream – are right for any occasion, from everyday meals for family and friends to special events when you want to impress. And, because cold mousses can be made ahead, they're perfect for entertaining.

REAL CHOCOLATE MOUSSE

🥄 8-10 servings
⏲ Can be made day before and kept in refrigerator

4 egg yolks
450 ml/ ³/₄ pint milk
60 g/2 oz caster sugar
1 tablespoon powdered gelatine
225 g/8 oz plain chocolate, chopped
450 ml/ ³/₄ pint double or whipping cream
Whipped cream and finely chopped pistachios (see right) to decorate

1 In large non-stick saucepan, beat egg yolks, milk and sugar until blended. Evenly sprinkle gelatine over mixture; leave to stand for 5 minutes to soften gelatine slightly. Stir in chopped chocolate.

2 Cook over low heat, stirring frequently with wooden spoon, for about 15 minutes or until gelatine dissolves completely, chocolate melts and mixture thickens and coats the spoon well (do not boil or mixture will curdle).

3 Pour mixture into bowl; cover and refrigerate until mixture mounds slightly when dropped from a spoon, about 1½ hours, stirring occasionally.

4 In medium bowl, whip double or whipping cream until stiff peaks form. With rubber spatula or wire whisk, fold whipped cream into chocolate mixture.

5 Pour mousse into 8-10 individual soufflé dishes or 1 large serving bowl; cover and refrigerate for 4 hours or until mousse is set.

6 Before serving, decorate mousse with whipped cream and finely chopped pistachios.

Piping whipped cream: *using piping bag with medium star tube, pipe whipped cream in shell shape at edge of each chocolate mousse.*

Chopping pistachios: *with sharp knife, on cutting board, finely chop shelled pistachios. Use to sprinkle over whipped cream and chocolate mousse.*

Chopped pistachios and whipped cream add flavour as well as colour to this wickedly rich chocolate mousse

RASPBERRY LAYERED MOUSSE

8 servings
Can be made day before and kept in refrigeraor

450 g/1 lb frozen raspberries

175-225 g/6-8 oz caster sugar

2 tablespoons powdered gelatine

2 eggs

300 ml/ $^{1}/_{2}$ pint milk

600 ml/1 pint double or whipping cream

14 ginger nut biscuits, crushed (about 150 g/5 oz)

Raspberries and mint leaves to decorate

1 Sprinkle raspberries with half of the sugar; set aside to thaw.

2 Place sieve over non-stick saucepan. With back of spoon, press and scrape raspberries and juice through sieve to purée; discard pips.

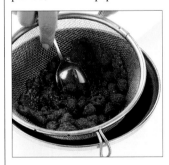

3 Sprinkle half of the gelatine over raspberry purée in saucepan; leave to stand for 5 minutes in order to allow gelatine to soften slightly.

4 Over medium heat, cook raspberry mixture until gelatine dissolves completely, stirring frequently.

5 Pour into bowl, cover and refrigerate until mixture mounds slightly when dropped from a spoon, about 1 $^{1}/_{2}$ hours, stirring occasionally.

6 Meanwhile, in another non-stick saucepan, beat eggs, milk and half of the remaining sugar until blended. Evenly sprinkle remaining gelatine over mixture; leave to stand for 5 minutes in order to soften gelatine slightly.

7 Cook gelatine mixture over low heat, stirring frequently, for 10 minutes or until gelatine dissolves completely and mixture coats a spoon well (do not boil or it will curdle).

8 Pour into bowl, cover and refrigerate until mixture mounds slightly when dropped from a spoon, about 1 $^{1}/_{2}$ hours, stirring occasionally.

9 About 10 minutes before gelatine mixtures are ready, in large bowl, whip double or whipping cream with remaining sugar until stiff peaks form.

10 With rubber spatula or wire whisk, gently fold half of the whipped cream into each of the gelatine mixtures.

11 In large serving bowl, layer half of the biscuits, then custard cream, rest of biscuits, then raspberry cream. Cover and refrigerate until set, about 3 hours.

> ### TO SERVE
> Decorate mousse with raspberries and mint leaves.

The different layers of Raspberry Layered Mousse can be seen if the dessert is made in a glass bowl

ORANGE LIQUEUR SOUFFLÉ

🍴 6 servings
⏱ Allow 2 hours preparation and cooking time

60 g/2 oz butter
50 g/1 ²/₃ oz plain flour
350 ml/12 fl oz milk
45 g/1 ¹/₂ oz caster sugar, plus extra for sprinkling
4 egg yolks
5 tablespoons orange liqueur
1 tablespoon grated orange zest
6 egg whites
Icing sugar for sprinkling
Whipped cream for serving (flavoured with orange liqueur or orange juice if liked)

1 In large non-stick saucepan over low heat, melt butter; stir in flour until blended. Gradually stir in milk; cook, stirring constantly, until mixture boils and thickens; boil for 1 minute.

2 Remove saucepan from heat. With wire whisk, beat caster sugar into milk mixture. Rapidly beat in egg yolks all at once until well mixed. Cool mixture to lukewarm, stirring occasionally. Stir in orange liqueur and grated orange zest.

3 Brush inside of 1.2 litre/2 pint soufflé dish with butter; sprinkle lightly with caster sugar.

If you sprinkle inside of buttered soufflé dish with caster sugar it will melt during baking and soufflé will not stick to dish

4 Preheat oven to 190°C/375°F/gas 5. In large bowl, with electric mixer on full speed, beat egg whites until stiff peaks form. With rubber spatula or wire whisk, gently fold beaten egg whites, one-third at a time, into egg yolk mixture.

5 Spoon mixture into prepared dish. With back of metal spoon, about 2.5 cm/1 inch from edge, make 4 cm/1¹/₂ inch deep indentation all round in soufflé mixture (centre will rise slightly higher than edge, making top hat effect when soufflé is done).

Making indentation in soufflé mixture for top hat effect

6 Bake soufflé for 30-35 minutes until knife inserted under top hat comes out clean.

7 When soufflé is done, remove from oven and sprinkle top lightly with sifted icing sugar; serve immediately. Hand whipped cream in bowl to spoon on to each serving, if you like.

The 'top hat' effect of this baked soufflé is created by making an indentation with a spoon in soufflé mixture before cooking

SUCCESSFUL SWEET SOUFFLÉS

Hot sweet soufflés consist of a thick sauce of butter, flour, milk, sugar, egg yolks and flavourings folded with stiffly beaten egg whites. For success every time, follow these simple guidelines.

• Always cook butter and flour first, to get rid of the raw taste of uncooked flour. When adding milk, take care to do it very gradually.

• Boil milk mixture for 1 minute so that smooth sauce is formed.

• Beat in egg yolks vigorously with pan off the heat.

• Fold egg whites gently into sauce, taking care not to stir whites.

• Bake soufflé on rack slightly below centre of oven so that mixture itself is centred and has sufficient room to rise.

• Do not open oven door before end of baking time; cold air could cause soufflé to fall.

FRESH APPLE SOUFFLÉ

🍴 4 servings
⏲ Allow about 1 hour preparation and cooking time

3 medium-sized cooking apples (about 450 g/1 lb)

45 g/1 ¹/₂ oz caster sugar

¹/₂ teaspoon almond essence

5 egg whites

Icing sugar for sprinkling

1 Peel apples; cut into quarters; with sharp knife, remove cores.

2 Cut apples into bite-sized chunks. In large saucepan over high heat, heat apples and *4 tablespoons water* to boiling. Reduce heat to low; cover and simmer for 8-10 minutes, stirring occasionally, until apples are tender. Stir in caster sugar and almond essence. Pour apple mixture into bowl; set aside to cool.

3 Preheat oven to 230°C/450°F/gas 8. In large bowl, with electric mixer on full speed, beat egg whites until stiff peaks form.

4 With rubber spatula or wire whisk, gently fold egg whites into cooled apple mixture until evenly incorporated.

5 Spoon mixture into 1.5 litre/2 ¹/₂ pint soufflé dish. Bake for 15 minutes or until soufflé is puffy and lightly browned. Remove soufflé from oven; sift icing sugar lightly over top and serve immediately.

Although not strictly speaking a soufflé, this simple, low-calorie dessert of apples, sugar and egg whites has a similar light and fluffy texture

CUSTARDS AND CREAMS

Velvety smooth, soft and pleasing, custards and creams are easy and quick to make. Most can be prepared ahead, making them excellent for menus in which other dishes require last-minute attention. Fruit Fools are the exception; they must be made just before serving, but preparation takes only about 20 minutes. In these pages you will find desserts ranging from simple family favourites like Crème Caramel to sophisticated party desserts like Zuccotto.

AMERICAN CREAM POTS

6 servings
Can be made day before (up to end of step 6) and kept in refrigerator

4 eggs

600 ml/1 pint milk

45 g/1 ½ oz caster sugar

1 teaspoon vanilla essence

6 tablespoons maple syrup

1 x 315 g/11 oz can mandarin orange segments, drained, to decorate

1 In large jug or bowl, with wire whisk, beat eggs, milk, sugar and vanilla essence until well blended.

2 Pour milk mixture into six 175 ml/6 fl oz mousse pots.

3 Arrange mousse pots in 30 cm/12 inch frying pan; fill pan with water to come halfway up sides of pots. Cover pan.

4 Over medium heat, heat water in pan to boiling point.

5 Simmer custards about 10 minutes or until beginning to set around edges. Remove pan from heat, then leave custards to stand in covered pan for 15 minutes until fully set.

6 Remove pots of custard from pan; refrigerate until well chilled, about 2 hours. If not serving immediately, cover each chilled dessert tightly and refrigerate.

7 Just before serving, pour 1 tablespoon maple syrup on top of each pot of custard.

8 To serve, top each custard with mandarin orange segments.

Maple syrup and canned mandarins are a quick and clever 'American' way to dress up a simple egg custard

CHOCOLATE CUPS

8 servings

Allow about 2 hours preparation and chilling time

175 g/6 oz plain chocolate flavour cake covering, broken into pieces

300 ml/ 1/2 pint double or whipping cream

1 x 400 g/400 ml can Devon custard

Few drops of orange food colouring (optional)

1 large banana

Cocoa powder

1 Place paper cake cases in each of eight 6 cm/2 1/2 inch holes in deep bun tin.

2 In small bowl set over saucepan of gently simmering water, gently heat chocolate cake covering, stirring frequently, until melted and smooth.

3 Starting from top rim of each paper case, carefully drizzle melted chocolate cake covering, 1 teaspoon at a time, down inside of case. About 3-4 teaspoons of melted chocolate will line each paper case.

4 If necessary, spread chocolate over inside of case with back of teaspoon.

5 Refrigerate until firm, about 30 minutes. With cool hands, remove 1 cake case at a time from refrigerator; gently but quickly peel paper case from each one, leaving chocolate cup.

6 Place empty chocolate cups on chilled dessert platter and refrigerate.

7 In small bowl, whip double or whipping cream until stiff peaks form.

8 With rubber spatula or wire whisk, fold whipped cream into custard until blended. Add food colouring, if used.

9 Slice banana and divide equally between cups. Spoon filling into cups. Refrigerate for at least 30 minutes or until filling is well chilled.

> *TO SERVE*
> *Lightly sprinkle cocoa through small sieve over creamy filling in Chocolate Cups.*

Beneath this creamy custard is a surprise filling of sliced banana

CRÈME CARAMEL

🍴 6 servings

🕐 Can be made day before and kept in refrigerator

120 g/4 oz granulated sugar

5 eggs

60 g/2 oz caster sugar

Few drops of vanilla essence

750 ml/1 ¼ pints milk

Cracked Caramel (page 119), Cape gooseberries or lime julienne and citrus fruit segments to decorate

1 Preheat oven to 150°C/300°F/gas 2. Put granulated sugar and *4 tablespoons water* in heavy saucepan and dissolve over low heat. Bring to the boil; boil, without stirring, until syrup is pale golden brown. Remove from heat and quickly pour into 6 small ramekins, or oval- or heart-shaped moulds.

2 Mix the eggs, caster sugar and vanilla essence together in a large bowl.

3 Warm milk in saucepan over low heat until it is hand hot, then pour it on to egg mixture, stirring constantly.

4 Brush butter on sides of ramekins or moulds above caramel. Strain custard into ramekins or moulds and place in a roasting tin. Pour in hot water to come halfway up sides of ramekins or moulds.

5 Bake in oven for about 45-60 minutes until set. Remove from oven and leave to cool, then refrigerate until set and well chilled, at least 12 hours or overnight.

6 Just before serving, loosen custards from ramekins or moulds with small knife. Turn each custard out on to a chilled dessert plate, letting syrup drip over custard and down sides. Add decoration of your choice.

Cracked Caramel

Cracked Caramel Decoration: *with end of rolling pin, carefully crack hardened caramel into small pieces.*

Cape Gooseberry Decoration *(also called physalis and Chinese lantern): carefully peel back inedible husk to resemble flower petals.*

Lime Julienne Decoration: *with vegetable peeler, remove zest from lime, leaving bitter white pith behind. Cut zest into fine strips.*

Lime Julienne

Cape Goosebе

CRÈME BRÛLÉE

- 6 servings
- Can be made day before up to end of step 3

Crème Brûlée

600 ml/1 pint single cream
4 eggs
60 g/2 oz caster sugar
1/2 teaspoon vanilla essence
45 g/1 1/2 oz demerara sugar

To serve

Cut-up fresh fruits (strawberries, pineapple and banana)
Canned mandarin-orange segments
Fresh mint sprigs

1 Preheat oven to 150°C/300°F/gas 2.

2 Blend cream, eggs, caster sugar and vanilla in large bowl. Pour into baking dish.

3 Stand dish in roasting tin containing 2.5 cm/1 inch hot water; bake in oven for about 1 hour or until just firm. Leave to cool, then refrigerate for at least 4 hours.

4 About 1 hour before serving, preheat grill to high. Work demerara sugar through sieve over chilled cream mixture.

5 Brown under a hot grill for 3-4 minutes until sugar has melted. The melted sugar will form a crisp crust over custard. If crust is done too early, the sugar will become soft and lose its crisp texture. Leave to cool.

6 To serve, arrange some sliced fruit in centre of Crème Brûlée with mint sprigs. Serve remaining fruit separately.

Working demerara sugar through sieve so it will be free of lumps; it should then brown evenly under the grill

To serve Crème Brûlée, tap top with metal spoon to crack crust and reveal creamy custard underneath

BRÛLÉE TOPPING

If your grill isn't very efficient and you find cult to get an even layer of brûlée on the custard cream, instead of sprinkling over the top of the custard and br the grill, try this alternative

Caramel Topping
Make a caramel as you would for crème caramel: put *90 g /3 oz granulated sugar* and *3 tablespoons water* in a heavy saucepan and heat gently until the sugar has dissolved. Bring to the boil without til the

DECORATING WITH SAUCES

There's more to serving a sauce than just spooning it over a pudding. It can be made into an eye-catching decoration that's quick and surprisingly easy to do; all that's needed is a bit of imagination coupled with a steady hand.

Fruit purées, bottled fruit and chocolate syrups, custard, cream and sweet sauces can all be used effectively.

The designs on these two pages should help to get you started. Each combines two different ingredients of contrasting colour yet compatible flavour. Choose from a wide variety of ingredients – colourful fruit sauces and purées, glistening jams and jellies, rich dark chocolate, golden custard.

Cream Wisps
Spoon raspberry purée on to plate. With small writing tube, pipe dots of double cream in a circle 2.5 cm/1 inch in from edge of purée. Draw tip of knife or skewer through 1 edge of each dot to form the shape of a wisp. Use to frame scoops of ice creams and sorbets.

Chocolate Spider Web
Spoon lightly whipped cream on to plate. With small writing tube, pipe 2 concentric circles of chocolate syrup or melted and cooled chocolate on to cream. With tip of knife or skewer, quickly draw lines in spoke fashion; alternate direction of each spoke, first from centre to edge, then from edge to centre. Use as a decoration for moulded desserts and individual portions of cakes and tarts.

Chocolate Chevrons

*Spoon custard on to plate. With small writing tube, pipe
parallel lines of chocolate syrup on to custard. Draw tip of
knife or skewer quickly across lines, first in 1 direction, then
in the other. Use as a decoration for scoops of ice cream.*

Cream Hearts

*Spoon strawberry purée on to plate. With small
writing tube, pipe dots of double cream in a circle
2.5 cm/1 inch in from edge of purée, and in heart
shape in centre. Draw tip of knife or skewer
through dots to make heart shapes. Use as
decoration for poached fruit.*

Cream Sunburst

*Spoon chocolate custard on to plate.
With small writing tube, pipe semi-
circular lines of double cream at
regular intervals. Starting at
smallest circle, draw tip of knife or
skewer across lines,
towards edge of plate. Use as a
decoration for individual portions of
sweet pies and tarts.*

On Raspberry Pond

*With small writing tube, pipe free-form
decorative shape of seedless raspberry jam on
to plate. Carefully spoon in double or
whipping cream to fill shape. If you like, add
fruit and mint leaves. Use as a decoration for
fresh fruit and fruit salads.*

ZUCCOTTO (FLORENTINE CREAM CAKE)

This delicious dessert comes from Italy, where it is traditionally made in a special pumpkin-shaped mould (zuccotto means 'little pumpkin' in Italian). Here *a large glass mixing bowl is used, and it works just as well as a special zuccotto mould, giving an equally good shape, as you can see in the photograph.*

Turned out upside-down, this luscious dinner party dessert looks pumpkin-shaped, which is why the Italians call it 'zuccotto', or 'little pumpkin'

4 Beat melted chocolate into butter and sugar mixture with remaining liqueur until smooth, thick and creamy.

5 In small bowl, whip 300 ml/ ½ pint double cream with 2 teaspoons coffee essence until stiff peaks form. Fold in grated chocolate.

6 Cover cake triangles in bowl with whipped cream mixture.

8-10 servings
Can be made day before and kept in refrigerator

1 Madeira cake, measuring about 23 x 12.5 cm/ 9 x 5 inches

6 tablespoons almond liqueur

135 g/4 ½ oz plain chocolate

120 g/4 oz icing sugar, sifted

60 g/2 oz butter, softened

450 ml/ ¾ pint double cream

4 teaspoons coffee essence

2 tablespoons slivered almonds, chopped

30 g/1 oz caster sugar

1 Line medium-sized bowl with cling film. Cut Madeira cake into 1 cm/ ½ inch thick slices; cut each slice diagonally in half to make 2 triangles.

2 Sprinkle 3 tablespoons almond liqueur on triangles of cake. Line bowl with triangles; reserve remaining triangles.

3 Break 90 g/3 oz chocolate into pieces and melt in bowl over pan of gently simmering water. Coarsely grate remaining chocolate. In bowl, beat icing sugar and softened butter until creamy.

Covering cake in bowl with whipped cream mixture

7 Spoon chocolate and almond liqueur mixture into centre of dessert and smooth top.

8 Neatly cover top of dessert with remaining cake triangles.

9 Cover bowl and refrigerate for at least 4 hours.

10 Meanwhile, in small saucepan over medium heat, cook chopped slivered almonds until golden, stirring frequently; cool.

11 In small bowl, whip remaining double cream with caster sugar and remaining 2 teaspoons coffee essence until soft peaks form.

12 Turn dessert out on to chilled platter; discard cling film. Cover dessert with whipped cream; sprinkle toasted chopped almonds on top.

DECORATIVE FINISHES FOR ZUCCOTTO

You can decorate the Zuccotto very simply, with toasted chopped almonds as in the main photograph (page 18), or you can sift cocoa powder or icing sugar over the top for an equally attractive finish. Another more decorative idea, which echoes the almond and coffee flavours of the Zuccotto, is this Daisy Design, and it only takes a few extra minutes to do.

Daisy Design
A simple daisy made from blanched or toasted almonds and chocolate 'coffee beans' is quick and effective to make: gently press 'coffee bean' into whipped cream icing for centre of daisy, then press slivered almonds round sweet for petals. If you like, make 1 large daisy centred on top of Zuccotto, or several small daisies placed round sides.

Toasted slivered almond

Slivered blanched almond

Chocolate 'coffee bean'

TO SERVE
Cut Zuccotto into slices and arrange on dessert plates to reveal different layers inside.

STRAWBERRY ORANGE CHARLOTTE

🍴 8 servings

⏱ Can be made day before and kept in refrigerator

2 tablespoons powdered gelatine

175 ml/6 fl oz orange juice

4 egg yolks

350 ml/12 fl oz milk

1 x 400 g/14 oz can sweetened condensed milk

225 g/8 oz frozen strawberries

60 g/2 oz caster sugar

4 tablespoons strawberry jam

4 tablespoons orange liqueur

25 g/ ³/4 oz cornflour

2 x 100 g/3 ¹/2 oz packets sponge fingers (boudoir biscuits)

450 ml/ ³/4 pint double or whipping cream

1 tablespoon icing sugar

Strawberries to decorate

1 In non-stick saucepan, sprinkle gelatine over orange juice; leave to stand for 5 minutes. Cook over medium heat until gelatine dissolves, stirring often.

2 In medium bowl, with wire whisk, beat egg yolks, milk and condensed milk until blended. Beat egg yolk mixture gradually into gelatine mixture. Cook over medium-low heat, stirring constantly, until mixture thickens and coats a spoon well, about 15 minutes (do not boil or it will curdle).

3 Pour custard mixture into large bowl; cover and refrigerate until mixture mounds slightly when dropped from a spoon, about 1 ¹/2 hours, stirring occasionally.

4 Meanwhile, sprinkle strawberries with caster sugar; thaw. In food processor or blender, blend strawberries and their juice with jam until smooth.

5 Pour mixture into medium saucepan; stir in liqueur, cornflour and 4 tablespoons water. Cook over medium-high heat, stirring constantly, until mixture boils and becomes thick; boil for 1 minute. Remove from heat.

6 Line bottom and sides of 23 cm/9 inch springform cake tin with sponge fingers.

7 If necessary, trim sponge fingers to fit tin so they will line bottom and stand upright round sides. Brush sponge fingers on bottom of tin with 4 tablespoons strawberry mixture (see Box, below). Cover tin tightly; set aside. Pour remaining strawberry mixture into bowl; allow to cool, stirring mixture occasionally.

8 In small bowl, whip 350 ml/12 fl oz double or whipping cream until stiff peaks form. With rubber spatula or wire whisk, fold whipped cream into custard mixture.

9 Spoon half of the custard mixture over sponge fingers in bottom of springform tin. Spoon 150 ml/ ¹/4 pint of strawberry mixture over custard layer. Add remaining custard mixture (see Box, below). Drop heaping spoonfuls of remaining strawberry mixture on top of custard. Using palette knife, swirl mixtures together to create a marbled design (see Box, below). Refrigerate until firm, at least 4 hours or overnight.

10 When ready to serve, carefully remove side of springform tin from charlotte; place charlotte on cake plate or stand. In small bowl, whip remaining double or whipping cream with sifted icing sugar until stiff peaks form. Spoon into piping bag with medium star tube; pipe in pretty design round top edge of charlotte. Cut strawberries in half and use to decorate charlotte attractively.

MAKING MARBLED DESIGN

Brushing sponge fingers on bottom of tin: *evenly spread 4 tablespoons strawberry mixture over sponge fingers.*

Adding custard mixture: *over second layer of strawberry mixture, spoon remaining custard mixture.*

Swirling mixtures: *with palette knife, swirl custard and strawberry mixtures together.*

Attractively swirled marbled design

TIRAMISÙ

10 servings

Can be made day before and kept in refrigerator

450 g/1 lb mascarpone cheese (see Box, below right)

75 g/2 ½ oz icing sugar, sifted

125 ml/4 fl oz coffee liqueur

90 g/3 oz plain chocolate, grated

450 ml/ ¾ pint double or whipping cream

2 teaspoons coffee essence

18 sponge fingers (boudoir biscuits)

1 In large bowl, with wire whisk or fork, beat mascarpone cheese, 60 g/2 oz icing sugar, 3 tablespoons coffee liqueur and two-thirds of grated chocolate. (Set aside remaining chocolate for top of dessert.)

2 In small bowl, whip 300 ml/½ pint double or whipping cream until stiff peaks form. With rubber spatula or wire whisk, fold cream into cheese mixture.

3 In small bowl, stir coffee essence, remaining coffee liqueur and 2 tablespoons water.

4 Place 4 sponge fingers in bottom of large glass bowl; brush with 2 tablespoons of coffee essence mixture. Spoon one-third of cheese mixture over sponge fingers. Repeat with sponge fingers, coffee essence mixture and cheese mixture to make 2 more layers. Top with remaining sponge fingers, gently pressing them into cheese mixture. Brush sponge fingers with remaining coffee essence mixture. Sprinkle remaining grated chocolate over dessert, reserving 1 tablespoon for decoration.

5 In small bowl, whip remaining cream with remaining icing sugar until stiff peaks form.

Sweetened mascarpone cheese, cream and coffee liqueur are layered with coffee-soaked sponge fingers in this heady Italian dessert

6 Spoon whipped cream into piping bag with large star tube. Pipe large rosettes on top of dessert.

7 Sprinkle reserved grated chocolate over whipped cream rosettes. Leave dessert in refrigerator until chilled and flavours are blended (this will take at least 4 hours).

TO SERVE
Serve Tiramisù well chilled in a glass serving bowl so that its different layers can be seen.

Large rosettes of whipped cream look good piped round edge of dish and sprinkled with grated chocolate

MASCARPONE CHEESE

Mascarpone, a fresh, double-cream cheese, is one of the great Italian cheeses available in cheese shops, delicatessens and many supermarkets.
It is buttery-smooth in texture and slightly nutty or tangy in flavour. As well as being used in recipes, it is superb with fresh seasonal fruit or fruit purées.

Mascarpone Cheese Substitute

If mascarpone cheese is not available when making Tiramisù, substitute *450 g/1 lb full-fat soft cheese, softened*; in step 1, in large bowl, with electric mixer or hand whisk, beat soft cheese and *3 table-spoons milk* until mixture is smooth and fluffy. Increase amount of icing sugar for cheese mixture to 80 g/2 ¾ oz; beat in with coffee liqueur, then stir in grated chocolate until evenly blended.

FRUIT FOOLS

4 servings (each flavour)
Allow about 20 minutes preparation for each flavour

PEACH

3 medium-sized ripe peaches

30 g/1 oz caster sugar

300 ml/ 1/2 pint double or whipping cream

1/8 teaspoon almond essence

Mint leaves to decorate

1 Peel, halve and stone peaches. Reserve 1 peach half for decoration. Cut remaining peaches into chunks.

2 In food processor or blender at medium speed, blend peach chunks and sugar together until smooth.

3 In small bowl, whip double or whipping cream together with almond essence until stiff peaks form.

4 With rubber spatula or wire whisk, fold almond-flavoured whipped cream into peach purée.

> ### TO SERVE
> Spoon mixture into parfait glasses or dessert dishes; decorate with reserved fruits and mint leaves.

RASPBERRY

225 g/8 oz frozen raspberries

60 g/2 oz caster sugar

300 ml/ 1/2 pint double or whipping cream

1/8 teaspoon almond essence

Raspberries and mint leaves to decorate

1 Sprinkle raspberries with sugar; set aside to thaw. Over large bowl, with back of spoon, press and scrape thawed raspberries with their juice firmly against medium-mesh sieve to purée; discard pips left in sieve.

2 In small bowl, whip double or whipping cream together with almond essence until stiff peaks form.

3 With rubber spatula or wire whisk, fold almond-flavoured whipped cream into raspberry purée.

Raspberry Fool

Peach Fool

KIWI FRUIT

3 large kiwi fruit

30 g/1 oz caster sugar

300 ml/ 1/2 pint double or whipping cream

1/8 teaspoon vanilla essence

Mint leaves to decorate

1 Peel kiwi fruit. Cut 1 kiwi fruit crossways in half. Reserve 1 half for decoration. Cut remaining kiwi fruit into chunks.

2 In food processor or blender at medium speed, blend kiwi fruit chunks and sugar together until smooth.

3 In small bowl, whip double or whipping cream together with vanilla essence until stiff peaks form.

4 With rubber spatula or wire whisk, fold vanilla-flavoured whipped cream into kiwi fruit purée.

Kiwi Fruit Fool

CHOCOLATE BOX WITH BERRIES AND CREAM

This spectacular, luscious-looking dessert is simple to make when you follow the easy step-by-step directions below, yet your guests cannot fail to be impressed with your apparently expert skills. The striking combination of rich dark chocolate with the lightness of the fresh strawberries and cream gives an opulent appearance which makes this dessert the perfect choice for any special occasion or celebration.

6 servings

Can be made day before (up to end of step 6) and kept in refrigerator

175 g/6 oz plain chocolate flavour cake covering, broken into pieces

30 g/1 oz cocoa powder

175 g/6 oz full-fat soft cheese, softened

60 g/2 oz butter, softened

175 g/6 oz icing sugar, sifted

2 tablespoons milk

450 ml/ 3/4 pint double or whipping cream

700 g/1 1/2 lb strawberries

Mint leaves to decorate

1 Turn 23 cm/9 inch square baking tin upside down; mould foil over outside of tin to make a smooth box shape. Turn right way up and remove tin; place foil box inside tin and press out any wrinkles so chocolate box will come away from foil smoothly.

2 In small bowl over pan of gently simmering water, heat pieces of plain chocolate cake covering, stirring frequently, until melted and smooth.

3 Pour melted chocolate into foil-lined tin and swirl round sides and bottom, keeping edges as even as possible (see Box, below). Refrigerate for 1 minute, then swirl chocolate round inside of tin a second time, to reinforce sides of chocolate box. Refrigerate until firm, about 30 minutes.

4 Meanwhile, prepare filling: dissolve cocoa powder in *2-3 tablespoons boiling water.* In large bowl, with electric mixer, beat soft cheese and butter until smooth (do not use margarine or filling will be too soft to cut). Add icing sugar, cocoa and milk; beat until light and fluffy.

5 In small bowl, whip 350 ml/12 fl oz double or whipping cream until stiff peaks form. With rubber spatula or wire whisk, fold whipped cream into soft cheese mixture.

6 Remove chocolate box in foil from tin (see Box, below), then gently peel foil from sides and base. Place chocolate box on platter. Spread soft cheese filling evenly in chocolate box. Refrigerate until filling is well chilled and firm, about 2 hours.

7 In small bowl, whip remaining double or whipping cream until stiff peaks form. Spoon into piping bag fitted with large star tube.

8 Pipe whipped cream in 2.5 cm/1 inch wide border on filling inside chocolate box. Cut larger strawberries in half and arrange over entire top of soft cheese filling. Decorate top of dessert with mint leaves. Serve remaining strawberries with dessert.

MAKING CHOCOLATE BOX

Pouring chocolate: *slowly pour warm melted chocolate into foil-lined baking tin*

Swirling chocolate: *gently tilt tin from side to side so chocolate swirls round sides and bottom*

Removing chocolate box: *carefully lift foil to remove chocolate box from tin*

The combination of strawberries with long stalks and fresh mint leaves makes this sensational dessert look colourful and stunning

MERINGUES

Light and delicate, crisp and sweet, meringue serves as the case for a classic Pavlova, makes layers for gâteaux such as dacquoise, and becomes tiny shells to hold fillings of cream, fruit and frozen mixtures. Meringue can also be shaped into mushrooms, to make stunning petits fours, while small meringues, spooned or piped into dollops like whipped cream, can top puddings or decorate cakes and gâteaux – bake them as for Miniature Meringue Shells (page 28).

PAVLOVA

 8 servings

Can be made day before (up to end of step 4) and kept in cool place

3 egg whites

175 g/6 oz caster sugar

1 teaspoon vinegar

1 teaspoon cornflour

5 kiwi fruit

300 ml/ 1/2 pint double or whipping cream

1 Place a sheet of non-stick baking parchment on a baking sheet and mark a 20 cm/8 inch circle on it, using plate or cake tin as guide.

2 Preheat oven to 150°C/300°F/gas 2. In large bowl, with electric mixer on full speed, beat egg whites until soft peaks form. Gradually sprinkle in sugar, 1 tablespoon at a time, beating well after each addition. Blend vinegar with cornflour and whisk into egg whites with last spoonful of sugar.

3 Spread meringue on circle on baking parchment, building sides up higher than centre. Put in centre of oven, reduce heat to 140°C/275°F/gas 1 and bake for 1 hour or until pale cream in colour.

4 Turn oven off and leave Pavlova to cool completely in oven. When cool, carefully remove from baking sheet and place on serving plate.

5 With sharp knife, peel off skin and thinly slice kiwi fruit.

6 In small bowl, whip double or whipping cream until stiff peaks form.

TO SERVE
Spoon two-thirds of cream into meringue; reserve few kiwi fruit slices; arrange remainder on cream. Top with remaining cream and reserved kiwi fruit.

OTHER FRUIT TOPPINGS
Although kiwi fruit remains the classic topping for Pavlova, other fruits can be used instead. Combine any or all of the following fruits with kiwi fruit, or use them on their own.

- Halved strawberries.

- Peeled and sliced peaches or nectarines.

- Peeled and cubed papaya (pawpaw).

- Pineapple chunks.

Softly whipped cream

Thinly sliced kiwi fruit

Mouthwatering 'marshmallow' meringue

DATE AND WALNUT DACQUOISE

- 8 servings
- Can be made day before and kept in refrigerator

120 g/4 oz walnut pieces

150 g/5 oz stoned dates

5 egg whites

225 g/8 oz caster sugar

25 g/ ³/₄ oz cocoa powder

Mocha Butter Cream (see Box, above right)

Icing sugar for sprinkling

1 Set aside a few walnut pieces and a few dates to use for decoration later. Coarsely chop remaining walnuts and cut remaining dates into 1 cm/¹/₂ inch pieces.

2 In large frying pan over medium heat, toast chopped walnuts until golden brown, stirring occasionally; remove pan from heat.

3 Line 2 baking sheets with non-stick baking parchment or foil. Using 23 cm/9 inch round plate or cake tin as guide, mark 1 circle on baking parchment on each baking sheet; set aside.

4 In large bowl, with electric mixer on full speed, beat egg whites until soft peaks form. Gradually sprinkle in caster sugar, 1 tablespoon at a time, beating well after each addition until sugar dissolves completely and egg whites stand in stiff, glossy peaks.

Meringue layers made with chopped dates, walnuts and cocoa are sandwiched together with a rich mocha-flavoured butter cream

5 Preheat oven to 180°C/350°F/gas 4. In small bowl, with spoon, mix chopped dates with about 4 tablespoons meringue mixture to separate pieces. With rubber spatula, gently fold cocoa, date mixture and toasted chopped walnuts into remaining meringue mixture.

6 Inside each circle on baking parchment, spoon half of the meringue mixture; with palette knife, evenly spread meringue to cover entire circle. Place baking sheets with meringue on 2 oven racks; bake for 15 minutes. Switch baking sheets between racks so meringue browns evenly; bake for 15 minutes longer or until meringue layers are crisp on the outside, but still soft and chewy on the inside.

7 Cool meringues on baking sheets on wire racks for 10 minutes. With palette knife, carefully loosen meringues from baking sheets and transfer them to wire racks to cool completely. (If not assembling dessert immediately, meringue layers can be stored, covered, for 1 day.)

8 When meringues are cool, prepare Mocha Butter Cream.

Walnut and date topping – a clue to what is inside this luscious meringue gâteau

MOCHA BUTTER CREAM

In large bowl, with electric mixer, beat *450 g/1 lb icing sugar, sifted, 90 g/3 oz butter, softened, 45 g/1 ¹/₂ oz cocoa powder* and *5 tablespoons hot black coffee* until blended. Beat until butter cream has an easy spreading consistency, adding more coffee if necessary.

9 To assemble cake: place 1 meringue layer, flat side up, on cake plate. Cover evenly with Mocha Butter Cream; spread to 1 cm/ ¹/₂ inch of edge. Top with second meringue layer, flat side down; press down gently. Cover; refrigerate until filling is firm.

TO SERVE
Sift icing sugar over dacquoise; decorate with reserved walnuts and dates. While firm, cut into wedges, then leave to soften for 5 minutes.

MERINGUE SHAPES

MERINGUE SHELLS

🍴 6 shells
⏱ Can be made day before and kept in refrigerator

3 egg whites

175 g/6 oz caster sugar

1 Preheat oven to 140°C/275°F/gas 1.

2 Line large baking sheet with non-stick baking parchment or foil.

3 In large bowl, with electric mixer on full speed, beat egg whites until soft peaks form.

4 Add sugar to egg whites 1 tablespoon at a time, beating well after each addition until egg whites stand in stiff, glossy peaks.

5 Spoon meringue into large piping bag fitted with medium star tube. Pipe meringue into six 10 cm/4 inch rounds, about 2.5 cm/1 inch apart, on lined baking sheet.

6 Pipe remaining meringue in decorative star border round edge of each meringue round.

7 Bake meringues for 45 minutes. Turn oven off; leave meringues in oven for 45 minutes longer to dry completely.

8 Cool meringues on baking sheet on wire rack for 10 minutes. With palette knife, carefully loosen and remove meringues from baking sheet to wire rack and leave to cool completely.

9 If not using meringues immediately, store in tightly covered container.

MINIATURE MERINGUE SHELLS
Prepare meringue as for Meringue Shells (above), up to end of step 4. With medium writing tube, pipe into thirty 4 cm/1½ inch rounds on baking sheet lined with non-stick baking parchment. With teaspoon, shape into nests. Bake in oven for 30 minutes. Turn oven off; leave in oven for 30 minutes longer. Cool as above in step 8. Yield: 30 miniature shells.

MERINGUE MUSHROOMS

1 Preheat oven to 95°C/200°F/gas ¼. Line large baking sheet with non-stick baking parchment or foil. Prepare meringue as in Meringue Shells (left).

2 With large writing tube, pipe meringue on to baking sheet in 24 mounds, 4 cm/1 ½ inches in diameter, to resemble mushroom caps.

3 Pipe remaining meringue upright on to baking sheet in twenty-four 3 cm/1¼ inch lengths, to resemble stalks.

4 Bake for 1¾ hours. Turn oven off; leave meringues in oven for 30 minutes longer. Cool completely on baking sheet on wire rack.

5 Break *60 g/2 oz plain chocolate* into pieces, melt in small bowl over saucepan of gently simmering water, stirring frequently; cool slightly.

6 With tip of small knife, cut small hole in centre of underside of mushroom cap. Place a little melted chocolate in hole; spread underside of cap with chocolate.

7 Carefully insert pointed end of stalk into chocolate-filled hole in centre of underside of mushroom cap.

8 Repeat with remaining caps and stalks. Leave chocolate to dry and set, about 1 hour. Store in tightly covered container. Before serving, sift *cocoa powder* lightly over tops. Yield: 24 mushrooms.

Meringue Shells filled with ice cream or whipped cream, topped with a variety of different coloured fresh fruits, make glorious table centrepieces

Miniature Meringue Shells and Meringue Mushrooms make mouthwatering bite-sized petits fours

Pancakes and Crêpes

Pancakes can be folded, rolled or stacked, with or without a filling, to make a different dessert every time you serve them, or they can be enjoyed just as they are, with a simple sprinkling of caster sugar and a squeeze of lemon. One side is always browner than the other, so have the pale side up when you fold or roll the pancakes, so that the browner, more attractive side is visible.

FREEZING PANCAKES

Pancakes can be prepared and frozen up to 2 months ahead. After stacking pancakes, interleaving them with non-stick baking parchment, allow to cool, then wrap stack tightly in foil; label and freeze. Use within 2 months. To thaw, allow to stand, wrapped, at room temperature for about 2 hours.

PANCAKES

8-10 pancakes

120 g/4 oz plain flour

1 egg, beaten

300 ml/ ½ pint milk and water mixed

1 tablespoon salad oil

Oil for frying

1 Put flour in bowl and make a well in centre. Add egg and gradually stir in half of the milk and water mixture. Using a whisk, blend in flour from sides of bowl. Beat well until mixture is smooth. Stir in remaining liquid and oil.

A handy measuring cup gives you an equal amount of batter every time

2 With pastry brush, brush bottom of 17.5 cm/7 inch pancake pan and 25 cm/10 inch frying pan with oil.

3 Over medium heat, heat both pans.

Tilt pan to coat bottom evenly

4 Pour 3-4 tablespoons batter into pancake pan; tilt pan to coat bottom evenly. Cook pancake for 2 minutes or until top is set and underside slightly browned.

5 Using palette knife, work carefully round pancake to loosen it from pan.

6 Invert pancake into hot frying pan. Cook other side for about 30 seconds. While first pancake is cooking, start cooking another pancake in pancake pan.

7 Slide pancake on to non-stick baking parchment. Repeat until all batter is used, stacking pancakes, with non-stick baking parchment between them. Use immediately or wrap in foil and refrigerate or freeze.

CRÊPES SUZETTE

🍴 6 servings
🕐 Allow about 1 hour preparation and cooking time

12 pancakes (page 30)

1 large orange

60 g/2 oz butter

30 g/1 oz caster sugar

4 tablespoons orange liqueur

Orange slices and shredded orange zest to decorate

1 Prepare pancakes. (If using frozen pancakes, allow to stand, wrapped, at room temperature for about 2 hours until thawed.)

2 About 30 minutes before serving, grate ½ teaspoon zest from orange. Halve orange crossways; squeeze enough juice from orange halves to give 5 tablespoons.

3 Prepare sauce: in large frying pan or chafing dish, over low heat, place grated orange zest, juice, butter and sugar. Heat gently until butter melts.

4 Fold each pancake in half, then fold each one again into quarters.

5 Arrange pancakes in sauce in pan or chafing dish and heat through.

6 In very small saucepan over low heat, gently heat liqueur until warm; remove saucepan from heat. Ignite liqueur with match; pour flaming liqueur over pancakes.

FLAMBÉ

Flambé is the French word for flamed, and generally refers to foods that are bathed in flaming spirits, usually brandy, Cognac or high-proof liqueur. Flaming burns off some of the alcohol, and when the flames die down, the food, now deliciously flavoured, is ready to enjoy. Crêpes Suzette is one of the best-known desserts to use this classic French cooking technique, which is also used in Cherries Jubilee (see recipe below). Here are some tips for success.

• Use a frying pan or chafing dish, preferably a shallow one, to let more oxygen reach the flames and keep them alive longer so they burn off more alcohol.

• Serving dishes should be heatproof; do not use your fine crystal.

• Use wooden matches or long fireplace matches, not book matches, for igniting the spirit.

• Gently warm the spirit before igniting it. Heat it in a very small metal saucepan or ladle, over a low heat – such as a candle – until it is warm but not hot.

• Hold the lighted match over the spirit to ignite the vapours, then slowly pour the flaming spirit over the food. Or, if there isn't much liquid in the frying pan, pour the warm spirit into the pan (don't stir) and light it. Tilt the pan to keep the flames alive as long as possible.

• When the flames die, serve the food at once.

CHERRIES JUBILEE
Just before serving, scoop *vanilla ice cream* into 6 dessert bowls. In large frying pan or in chafing dish at the table, melt *300 g/10 oz redcurrant jelly*; stir until smooth. Add *one 425 g/15 oz can stoned black cherries, drained*; heat until simmering. Pour in *125 ml/4 fl oz brandy*; heat, without stirring, for 1 minute. Light brandy with match. Spoon flaming cherries over ice cream. Makes 6 servings.

TO SERVE
When flames die down, place pancakes on warm dessert plates; decorate with orange slices and shredded orange zest.

UPSIDE-DOWN APPLE PANCAKE

6 servings
Allow 40 minutes preparation and cooking time

3 large Golden Delicious apples

60 g/2 oz butter

1 teaspoon ground cinnamon

120 g/4 oz caster sugar

50 g/1²/₃ oz plain flour

5 tablespoons milk

¹/₂ teaspoon baking powder

4 eggs, separated

1 Peel and core apples; cut each apple into slices about 3 mm/¹/₈ inch thick.

2 Place large frying pan with all-metal handle over medium-low heat (if handle is not all metal, cover it with heavy-duty foil).

3 Put butter in frying pan (do not use margarine because it separates from sugar during cooking). Melt butter, then stir in cinnamon and 60 g/2 oz sugar; remove pan from heat.

4 In butter mixture in pan, arrange apple slices, overlapping them slightly (see Box, below). Repeat with smaller circle of apple slices in centre.

5 Return pan to low heat; cook for 10 minutes or until apples are tender but still crisp (see Box, below).

6 Meanwhile, preheat oven to 200°C/400°F/gas 6. In medium bowl, with fork, beat flour, milk, baking powder and egg yolks until blended; set aside.

If apple slices are arranged carefully in pan before cooking, they will turn out beautifully

7 In large bowl, with electric mixer on full speed, beat egg whites and remaining sugar until soft peaks have formed. With rubber spatula, very gently fold egg whites into egg yolk mixture.

8 Cover apple slices in pan with egg mixture (see Box, below); with rubber spatula, spread mixture evenly.

9 Bake pancake in oven for 10 minutes or until golden brown. Remove pan from oven and carefully invert pancake on to warm platter.

PLACING APPLES AND PANCAKE MIXTURE IN PAN

Arranging apple slices: round edge of pan, place apple slices in a circle. Do not crowd apple slices – overlap them slightly so they cook evenly.

Spoon pancake mixture carefully over apple slices or slices will be dislodged and spoil the look of the finished dessert

Testing apple slices: with prongs of fork, gently pierce apple slices. They are done when easy to pierce.

Covering apple slices: with large metal spoon, slowly pour egg mixture over apple slices, taking care not to shift them.

FRUIT DESSERTS

When eaten by itself at the peak of its freshness and flavour, fruit is truly a 'natural' dessert. But it can also be transformed into a myriad of different and delicious puddings, ranging from simple mixtures such as Gingered Fruit (below) to more elaborate preparations like Fresh Fruit Gâteau (page 40). Importing has extended the seasonal availability of many familiar fruits, and given us new and exotic kinds, to add flavour, colour and texture to desserts all year round.

GINGERED FRUIT

8 servings
Allow 1 ½ hours preparation and chilling time

2 x 425 g/15 oz cans apricot halves in syrup

1 x 475 g/17 oz can or jar figs in syrup

3 large Red Delicious apples

3 large pears

350 g/12 oz seedless red grapes

350 g/12 oz seedless green grapes

4 tablespoons chopped stem ginger in syrup

2 tablespoons lemon juice

1 Into large bowl, pour apricot halves with their syrup and figs with their syrup.

2 With sharp knife, cut unpeeled apples and pears into bite-sized chunks; discard cores.

3 Add apples and pears to fruit mixture in bowl with grapes, ginger and lemon juice; toss to mix well.

4 Cover and refrigerate for at least 1 hour to blend flavours.

This combination of fresh and canned fruits can be enjoyed all year round

FRUIT CONTAINERS

Many fruits come 'pre-packaged' in pretty casings which, once freed of their fillings, can be carved and cut for more spectacular servings.

The peel of melons and oranges can be given a scalloped edge, or formed into baskets, with or without a strip over the top for the handle; pineapples can be scooped out, part of their crowns intact, to make attractive 'fruit bowls', filled simply with their own chopped fruit to make easier eating.

Especially eye-catching effects are achieved by using contrasting fruits and shells: red fruits, such as watermelon and raspberries, stand out in green-fleshed melons, while rich green kiwi fruit contrasts well with the amber flesh of papaya in its shell; or for a more delicate effect, fill with mixed pastel-shaded balls of charentais, honeydew and watermelon.

Charentais Cup
Cut charentais melon cross-ways in half. Hollow out halves, then fill with balls of charentais, honeydew or Gallia and watermelon. For added colour, sprinkle with a few blueberries, then decorate with a small sprig of mint.

Gallia Bowl
Cut slice off top of Gallia melon; scoop out seeds from centre. Heap centre with watermelon balls and raspberries, allowing them to spill out over top of melon flesh.

Watermelon Basket
Into small round watermelon, make horizontal cut from each end 5 cm/2 inches from top (do not cut through); leave 2.5 cm/1 inch strip in centre. Then make two vertical cuts from top of melon down to horizontal cuts, to create handle. Scoop out melon. If you like, cut scalloped edge round rim of basket. Fill with watermelon, charentais, honeydew or Gallia melon balls, and decorate with sprigs of mint.

Papaya Boat
Slice papaya (pawpaw) lengthways in half. Remove seeds; scoop out flesh and cut into bite-sized chunks. Fill papaya halves with chunks of papaya and honeydew melon. Top with kiwi fruit triangles and decorate with sprig of mint.

Grapefruit Half
Cut grapefruit crossways through centre in zig-zag pattern. Scoop out sections. Fill with clementines in liqueur and raspberries. Decorate with sprig of mint.

Pineapple Boat
Cut pineapple lengthways in half. Cut out core and chunks of flesh. Cut thin slice from underside. Fill shell with kiwi fruit and pineapple; crown with strawberry half.

Filled Fruits
Cut deep 'X' in top of figs, kiwi fruit and strawberries (peel kiwi fruit first). Gently spread fruit apart to make 'petals'; pipe whipped cream into centre of each fruit.

POACHED PEARS

🍴 12 servings

⏱ Allow 4 ½ hours preparation and chilling time

1 x 1 litre/1 ³/₄ pint carton cranberry juice drink or diluted blackcurrant cordial

100 g/3 ½ oz caster sugar

1 medium-sized lemon, cut in half

12 medium-sized firm pears

2 tablespoons redcurrant jelly

Mint to decorate

1 In large flameproof casserole, combine fruit juice or cordial, sugar, lemon halves and *450 ml/ ³/₄ pint water.*

TO SERVE
Arrange pear halves in deep platter; pour syrup over pears. Decorate with mint leaves.

---

2 Peel 6 pears, being careful to leave their stalks attached.

3 With sharp knife, cut peeled pears length-ways in half. With teaspoon, scoop out cores and stringy portions from pear halves.

4 As each pear half is peeled and cored, place it in fruit juice mixture, turning to coat completely to help prevent pears from discolouring.

5 Over high heat, bring pear mixture to the boil. Reduce heat to low; cover and simmer for 10-15 minutes until pears are tender. With slotted spoon, transfer pear halves to large bowl.

6 Repeat same procedure (steps 2 to 5) with remaining 6 pears.

7 After all pears are poached, over high heat, bring fruit juice mixture in casserole to the boil; cook, uncovered, for about 20 minutes or until liquid is reduced to about 350 ml/12 fl oz.

PEARS
William's and Comice are the best varieties of pear for cooking.
 If you have a melon baller, you can use it to remove cores from pears easily and without waste, instead of a teaspoon. After scooping out core, run melon baller from core to stalk and blossom end of pear to remove stringy portion.
 To prevent peeled or chopped pears from browning if left to stand, sprinkle them with lemon juice.

---

8 Add redcurrant jelly to hot liquid; stir until dissolved. Pour hot syrup over pear halves in bowl; cool. Cover and refrigerate until pears are chilled, about 3 hours, turning them occasionally.

Stalks on some pear halves round edge of platter are left on to create interest

Pears have been poached in cranberry juice drink to colour them a delicate rosy pink

POACHED PEACHES IN ROSÉ WINE

6 servings

Can be made day before and kept in refrigerator

600 ml/1 pint rosé wine

8 lemon balm, geranium or bay leaves, plus extra for decoration

About 75 g/2 ¹/₂ oz caster sugar

Grated zest of 1 lemon

6 large peaches

1 In flameproof casserole into which peaches will fit snugly, mix wine, lemon balm, geranium or bay leaves, sugar, lemon zest and *450 ml/ ³/₄ pint water.*

2 Peel peaches (see Box, above right). Add peaches to wine mixture in casserole as soon as they are peeled to prevent discolouring.

PEELING PEACHES

1 Into saucepan of rapidly boiling water, with slotted spoon, dip peaches for about 15 seconds.

2 With slotted spoon, immediately transfer peaches to saucepan or bowl of cold water.

3 Lift peaches out of water; carefully peel off skins with sharp knife.

3 Over high heat, bring peaches and wine mixture to the boil. Reduce heat to low; cover and simmer for 5-10 minutes, shaking pan occasionally.

4 Spoon peaches and wine mixture into large bowl. Cover, then refrigerate for at least 6 hours or overnight. Discard leaves before serving.

Decorate peaches with fresh leaves to echo the flavour of those used in cooking

WINTER FRUIT COMPOTE

🍴 4 servings

⏲ Allow about 20 minutes preparation time

120 g/4 oz stoned prunes

120 g/4 oz dried apricot halves

125 ml/4 fl oz apple juice or orange juice

2 teaspoons light soft brown sugar

¹/₄ teaspoon ground cinnamon

1 large banana

Whipped Topping (see Box, right)

1 In medium saucepan over high heat, bring prunes, apricots, apple or orange juice, brown sugar and cinnamon to the boil.

2 Reduce heat to low; cover and simmer for 10 minutes, stirring fruit mixture occasionally.

3 Meanwhile, peel banana and cut into chunks 2.5 cm/1 inch thick. Prepare Whipped Topping.

4 Remove saucepan from heat. With rubber spatula, gently stir banana chunks into dried fruit mixture.

Stirring banana into dried fruit mixture

Dried fruits retain their shape if they are poached gently and not overcooked

WHIPPED TOPPING

In small bowl, with electric mixer, beat *4 tablespoons well-chilled evaporated milk* with *1 tablespoon sifted icing sugar* until stiff peaks form.

Evaporated milk beats better if partially frozen.

TO SERVE
Spoon warm fruit and Whipped Topping on to 4 dessert plates.

SUMMER FRUIT
WITH ALMOND CHANTILLY YOGURT

🍴 8 servings

⏱ Allow about 30 minutes preparation time

Almond Chantilly Yogurt (see Box, right)

4 large kiwi fruit

4 medium-sized plums

2 large peaches

2 medium-sized bananas

1 small charentais melon

120 g/4 oz raspberries

120 g/4 oz blueberries

120 g/4 oz blackberries

Lemon leaves and flaked almonds to decorate

1 Prepare Almond Chantilly Yogurt; spoon into small serving bowl. Cover and chill in refrigerator until ready to serve.

2 About 20 minutes before serving, with sharp knife, peel kiwi fruit; cut each one in half lengthways.

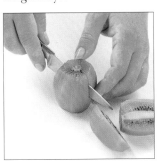

3 Cut each plum and peach in half; discard stones. Peel bananas; cut each in half crossways, then cut each half lengthways into 2 pieces.

4 With sharp knife, cut charentais melon into thin wedges; remove seeds and cut rind from each wedge.

5 Arrange prepared fruit decoratively on large platter. Top with raspberries, blueberries and blackberries.

TO SERVE
Decorate dessert with lemon leaves; decorate Almond Chantilly Yogurt with flaked almonds and serve to spoon over fruit.

FRESH FRUIT GÂTEAU

This spectacular showpiece is an artfully arranged selection of juicy, ripe charentais and honeydew melons, red and blue berries, kiwi fruit and pineapple. It makes a wonderful centrepiece for a summer buffet table, and is ideal for barbecues and other informal events when guests can serve themselves. It can be prepared ahead of time too, as long as it is kept, well wrapped, in the refrigerator until you are ready to serve. The calorie-conscious will find the combination of fruit flavours absolutely delicious when eaten plain, but for those who don't mind throwing caution to the wind, a dollop of Crème Cointreau will make it sweeter.

8-10 servings
Allow 3 hours preparation and chilling time

1 large charentais melon

1 medium-sized honeydew melon

1 large pineapple

2 large kiwi fruit

350 g/12 oz strawberries

225 g/8 oz blueberries

225 g/8 oz raspberries

Crème Cointreau (see Box, page 41)

Mint sprig to decorate

1 Cut each charentais and honeydew melon lengthways into 4 wedges. With spoon, scoop out seeds. Cut wedges crossways into 2.5 cm/1 inch thick slices; cut rind off each slice. Set aside.

2 Cut crown and skin off pineapple. Cut pineapple lengthways in half; cut crossways into 1 cm/½ inch thick slices. Cut out tough core of each slice. Cut about one-quarter of the pineapple slices into bite-sized pieces. Peel kiwi fruit; cut into wedges.

3 On large plate with rim (to catch any fruit juices), arrange half of the nice large honeydew slices round rim. Reserve small honeydew slices.

Arranging honeydew slices round edge of plate

ALTERNATIVE FRUIT ARRANGEMENT

Using only four different kinds of fresh fruit, you can create just as eye-catching an arrangement as in the main photograph on page 41. Neat wedges of charentais and honeydew melon can be combined with slices of fresh pineapple, with 'cherry blossoms' providing a pretty finishing touch.

Cherry Blossoms

Fresh mint leaf adds vibrant colour

Cherry is cut lengthways with stalk end left intact to form 'petals'

Four Fruit Gâteau

1 Cut *1 large charentais melon* lengthways into 3 wedges, and cut *1 medium-sized honeydew* lengthways into 4 wedges. With spoon, scoop out seeds. Cut wedges crossways into 2.5 cm/1 inch thick slices, then cut rind off each slice.

2 Cut crown and skin off *1 large pineapple*; reserve crown for decoration. Cut pineapple lengthways in half, then cut crossways into 2.5 cm/1 inch slices. Cut out tough core of each pineapple slice and discard.

3 On large round platter with rim (to catch any fruit juices), arrange large honeydew slices in a ring; fill centre of ring with end pieces; cut pieces to fit, if necessary. Repeat layering with charentais, pineapple and more honeydew slices, filling centre of ring with end fruit pieces as you assemble each layer.

4 Make Cherry Blossoms (see above) from *450 g/ 1 lb fresh cherries*; arrange on top of gâteau. Cover tightly and refrigerate for at least 1 hour or until ready to serve.

4 Arrange layers of pineapple slices in centre of plate.

5 Arrange half of the large charentais slices over honeydew slices on rim of plate. Reserve small charentais slices.

6 Repeat with another layer of honeydew and charentais slices. With remaining pineapple and reserved small melon slices, fill in any gaps. Place kiwi fruit wedges on top.

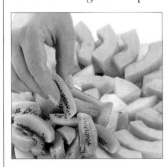

This gâteau isn't a gâteau at all – simply a clever arrangement of fruit in the shape of a cake!

7 Make neat piles of strawberries, blueberries, raspberries and bite-sized pieces of pineapple to cover rest of top of fruit gâteau.

8 Cover gâteau tightly; refrigerate for at least 1 hour or until ready to serve.

9 Meanwhile, prepare Crème Cointreau.

CRÈME COINTREAU
In medium bowl, whip *450 ml/³/₄ pint double or whipping cream* with *60 g/2 oz icing sugar, sifted*, just until soft peaks form. Gradually beat in *4 tablespoons orange liqueur.*

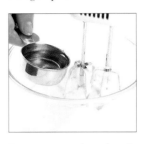

Spoon cream into bowl; cover and refrigerate until ready to serve.

Variegated mint is an unusual decoration for a dessert, but here it looks most effective perched on top of summer fruits

SHORTCAKE WITH FRUIT AND CREAM

Whipped cream and strawberries are the usual filling and topping for a traditional American summer shortcake; this deluxe version goes one step further, combining a variety of different coloured fresh fruits with sweetened whipped cream for a more dramatic effect. Of course you don't have to use the fruits suggested here, as long as you are careful to choose ripe, juicy fruits in season and aim for a good contrast of bright colours and interesting shapes and flavours. This fresh, attractive dessert is perfect to serve at an informal gathering with friends, such as at a summer brunch party or al fresco lunch.

8 servings
Allow 1 hour preparation and cooking time

2 large nectarines
45 g/1 ¹/₂ oz caster sugar
30 g/1 oz light soft brown sugar
190 g/6 ¹/₂ oz self-raising flour
90 g/3 oz butter
1 teaspoon baking powder
¹/₂ beaten egg
85 ml/3 fl oz milk
120 g/4 oz cherries
1 small kiwi fruit
225 g/8 oz blackberries or blueberries
300 ml/ ¹/₂ pint double or whipping cream

1 Cut nectarines in half and remove stones; slice. In medium bowl, toss nectarines with 1 tablespoon caster sugar. Cover and refrigerate.

2 Preheat oven to 230°C/450°F/gas 8. Grease 20 cm/8 inch round cake tin.

3 Make crumble topping: in small bowl, with fork, mix brown sugar and 40 g/1 ¹/₄ oz flour. With pastry blender or fingertips, cut or rub 30 g/1 oz butter into flour mixture until consistency of mixture resembles peas. Set aside.

MAKING SHORTCAKE

Spreading mixture: *in greased cake tin, with rubber spatula, evenly spread shortcake mixture.*

Sprinkling topping: *over mixture in tin, evenly sprinkle crumble topping.*

Sprinkle crumble topping evenly over shortbread so that it will brown nicely during baking

Testing if cooked: *when shortcake is golden, insert cocktail stick in centre; it should come out clean.*

Transferring to rack: *after removing from cake tin, place shortcake, crumble side up, on wire rack to cool.*

Handle shortcake gently so crumble topping is not dislodged

4 In large bowl, with fork, mix together baking powder, remaining flour and 1 tablespoon caster sugar.

5 With pastry blender or fingertips, cut or rub remaining butter into flour mixture until consistency of mixture resembles coarse crumbs.

6 In another small bowl, stir beaten egg into milk. Add egg and milk mixture all at once to flour mixture, then stir lightly together with fork until flour mixture is just moistened.

7 Spread shortcake mixture in tin and sprinkle with topping, then bake for 20 minutes or until golden (see Box, page 42). Cover with foil during last 5 minutes of baking if topping is browning too quickly.

8 Carefully remove shortcake from tin; transfer to wire rack (see Box, page 42); cool slightly, about 10 minutes. (Or cool completely to serve later.)

9 Reserve three cherries with stalks for decoration; remove stalks and stones from remaining cherries. Peel kiwi fruit; cut into bite-sized pieces. Gently stir stoned cherries, kiwi fruit and blackberries or blueberries into nectarine mixture.

10 In small bowl, whip double or whipping cream with remaining caster sugar until stiff peaks form.

11 With long serrated knife, carefully split shortcake in half horizontally.

12 Place bottom half of shortcake, cut side up, on dessert plate; top with all but about 60 g/2 oz fruit.

13 Spoon about two-thirds of whipped cream over top of fruit on shortcake.

Spooning whipped cream evenly over fruit so that it spills out over edge when shortcake is placed on top

14 Place top half of shortcake, crumble side up, on cream.

15 Pile reserved fruit in centre of shortcake. Top shortcake with remaining whipped cream and reserved cherries.

Luscious layers of fresh, juicy fruits, whipped cream and crumbly shortcake are topped with a trio of sweet red cherries

CAKES AND GÂTEAUX

There's a cake or gâteau in this section for every occasion, every feast day, every season. There are lavish cakes to glorify grand celebrations such as weddings, and simple cakes to accompany a cup of morning coffee or afternoon tea, or bring a family meal to a happy ending. The gâteaux are richer and more elaborate, ideal for dinner parties and other such special occasions. Most of the recipes in this section start 'from scratch', but Celebration Buffet Cake (page 62) cleverly turns packet sponge mix into a spectacularly delicious treat.

CINNAMON CREAM GÂTEAU

- 16 servings
- Can be made up to 3 days ahead and kept in refrigerator

175 g/6 oz soft margarine
100 g/3 ½ oz caster sugar
1 tablespoon ground cinnamon
1 egg
215 g/7 ½ oz plain flour
450 ml/ ³/4 pint double or whipping cream
Cocoa powder

1 Preheat oven to 190°C/375°F/gas 5. Tear 9 sheets of non-stick baking parchment, each about 21 cm/8 ½ inches long. On 1 sheet of baking parchment, trace circle, using base of 20 cm/8 inch round cake tin as a guide. Evenly stack all the baking parchment sheets with the marked sheet on top. With kitchen scissors, cut out rounds (see Box, above right).

2 In large bowl, combine margarine, sugar, cinnamon, egg and 150 g/5 oz flour. With electric mixer, beat ingredients until well mixed, constantly scraping bowl with rubber spatula. Continue beating until light and fluffy, about 3 minutes, occasionally scraping bowl. With spoon, stir in remaining flour to make a soft dough.

3 With wet cloth, dampen 1 large or 2 small baking sheets. Place 2 baking parchment rounds on large baking sheet, or 1 on each small baking sheet; with palette knife, spread 4 tablespoons dough in very thin layer on each round (see Box, right).

4 Bake for 6-8 minutes until lightly browned round the edges. Cool on baking sheet on wire rack for 5 minutes; with fish slice, carefully remove biscuit, still on paper, to wire rack to cool completely (see Box, right).

MAKING BISCUIT LAYERS

Cutting baking parchment rounds: holding stack of baking parchment sheets, with kitchen scissors, cut out nine 20 cm/8 inch rounds, using top marked sheet as guide.

Placing rounds on baking sheet: on dampened large baking sheet, place 2 baking parchment rounds, side by side. (Or place 1 round on 1 small baking sheet.)

Spreading dough on baking parchment: with palette knife, spread very thin, even layer of dough on each baking parchment round.

Transferring biscuit to wire rack: with fish slice, transfer biscuit, on parchment round, to wire rack.

Peeling off paper: with fingers, carefully peel baking parchment off each biscuit.

5 Let baking sheet cool before spreading parchment rounds with more dough. (The more baking sheets you have, the faster you can bake the biscuits.) Repeat until all dough is baked, to make 9 biscuits in all. If not assembling gâteau immediately, stack cooled biscuits carefully on flat plate; cover tightly and store in cool, dry place.

6 Early on day of serving, in medium bowl, whip cream until stiff peaks form.

7 Carefully peel parchment off 1 biscuit (see Box, page 44); place on cake plate. Spread with whipped cream. Repeat layering until all biscuits are used, ending with whipped cream.

8 Sift cocoa over whipped cream. If you like, with dull edge of knife, mark 16 wedges on top of gâteau. Refrigerate for at least 4 hours to let biscuits soften slightly for easier cutting.

GINGER CREAM GÂTEAU

If you like, you can change the flavour of this spectacular-looking gâteau from cinnamon to ginger.

Substitute *1 tablespoon ground ginger* for the ground cinnamon in the biscuit dough, then, for decoration, omit sprinkling whipped cream top with cocoa and instead make decorative pattern of finely chopped *crystallized ginger* on each marked wedge of gâteau.

Cocoa powder is sprinkled liberally over whipped cream on top of gâteau

After being sprinkled with cocoa, top of gâteau is marked into 16 wedges to make it easy to serve

Nine layers of crisp, cinnamon-flavoured 'biscuit' are sandwiched together with luscious whipped cream

DOUBLE CHOCOLATE MOUSSE CAKE

This luscious, rich mousse cake is the best chocolate dessert ever – dark, moist, very chocolatey, and soul satisfying! There is no flour in it; but the cake holds together beautifully when cut into slices for serving. Crystallized violets adorning the cream add an elegant finishing touch to the top of the cake.

8-10 servings

Can be made day before and kept in refrigerator

---

450 g/1 lb plain chocolate, broken into pieces

450 g/1 lb butter, cut into cubes

200 g/7 oz caster sugar

250 ml/8 fl oz single cream

8 eggs

Chocolate Glaze (see Box, page 47)

300 ml/½ pint double or whipping cream

Crystallized violets to decorate

1 Preheat oven to 180°C/350°F/gas 4. Grease 23 cm/9 inch springform cake tin.

2 In large heavy saucepan over low heat, heat chocolate, butter, sugar and single cream, stirring frequently, until chocolate melts and mixture is smooth.

3 In large bowl, with wire whisk or fork, beat eggs lightly; slowly beat warm chocolate mixture into eggs until well blended.

4 Pour mixture into spring-form tin so that it spreads evenly.

5 Bake for about 45 minutes or until skewer inserted in cake 5 cm/2 inches from edge comes out clean. Cool cake completely in tin on wire rack.

Pouring mixture into tin

> **TO SERVE**
> Decorate piped cream round top edge of cake with crystallized violets.

Ridged effect on chocolate glaze is made by swirling spatula over glaze while glaze is still warm

6 When cake is cool, carefully remove side of tin; wrap cake tightly, still on tin base, and refrigerate until it is well chilled, at least 6 hours.

7 Prepare Chocolate Glaze.

8 Line cake plate with strips of greaseproof paper. Unwrap cake; remove from tin base. Place cake on plate and spread with warm glaze (see Box, right). Discard greaseproof paper.

9 In small bowl, whip double or whipping cream until stiff peaks form. Spoon whipped cream into piping bag with medium star tube (see Box, right) and pipe cream round top edge of cake. Refrigerate cake if not serving immediately.

CHOCOLATE GLAZE

In heavy non-stick saucepan over very low heat, heat *175 g/6 oz plain chocolate chips* and *30 g/1 oz butter*, stirring frequently, until chocolate is melted and smooth. (If pan is too thin it will transfer heat too fast and burn chocolate.)

Remove pan from heat; beat in *3 tablespoons milk* and *2 tablespoons golden syrup.*

GLAZING AND DECORATING CAKE

Placing cake on plate: *on cake plate lined with strips of greaseproof paper (to catch glaze as it drips), carefully place well-chilled cake.*

Spreading glaze over cake: *with palette knife, evenly spread warm glaze over top and down side of cake.*

Don't worry if your cake sinks and looks unattractive at this stage; once glazed and decorated, it will look superb

Piping cream: *round top edge of cake, pipe scrolls of whipped cream to make continuous circle.*

Filling piping bag with cream: *into piping bag with medium star tube, spoon whipped cream. Twist end of bag to enclose cream.*

WALNUT CREAM GÂTEAU

10 servings

Can be made day before and kept in refrigerator

450 g/1 lb walnut pieces

50 g/1 ²/₃ oz self-raising flour

¹/₂ teaspoon baking powder

5 eggs, separated

150 g/5 oz caster sugar

2 tablespoons corn oil

600 ml/1 pint double or whipping cream

30 g/1 oz icing sugar, sifted

1 In food processor or blender, finely grind three-quarters of walnuts with flour and baking powder. (If using blender, blend ingredients in batches.)

2 Preheat oven to 180°C/350°F/gas 4. Grease two 23 cm/9 inch round cake tins; line bottoms of tins with non-stick baking parchment.

3 In large bowl, with electric mixer on full speed, beat egg whites until soft peaks form; gradually sprinkle in one-third of caster sugar, beating until sugar completely dissolves and whites stand in stiff peaks.

4 In another large bowl, with electric mixer, beat egg yolks, corn oil and remaining caster sugar until very thick and lemon-coloured, about 5 minutes. With rubber spatula or wire whisk, gently fold nut mixture and beaten egg whites into egg yolk mixture just until blended.

5 Spoon mixture into tins, spreading evenly. Bake for 20-25 minutes or until tops of cakes spring back when lightly touched with finger. Immediately loosen edges of cakes from sides of tins; turn out cakes on to wire racks and peel off baking parchment. Cool completely.

6 In large bowl, whip double or whipping cream with icing sugar until stiff peaks form. Spoon about one-quarter of whipped cream into piping bag with large star tube; reserve for decoration. Chop remaining walnuts for decoration.

7 With serrated knife, cut each cake in half horizontally to make 4 thin layers in all.

8 Place 1 cake layer on cake plate; spread with one-quarter of whipped cream.

9 Repeat layering, ending with a cake layer. Spread remaining one-quarter of whipped cream on side of cake.

10 Reserve 30 g/1 oz chopped walnuts; press remaining chopped walnuts into cream on side of cake. Pipe whipped cream in piping bag on top of cake in parallel lines.

11 Sprinkle reserved chopped walnuts in between lines of cream on top of cake.

Parallel lines of piped whipped cream are separated by chopped walnuts

12 Refrigerate cake if not serving immediately.

AUSTRIAN CHOCOLATE CAKE

🍴 8 servings

⏰ Can be made day before and kept in a cool place

250 g/9 oz plain chocolate, broken into pieces

175 g/6 oz unsalted butter

6 eggs, separated

200 g/7 oz caster sugar

30 g/1 oz self-raising flour

60 g/2 oz plain chocolate flavour cake covering

1 tablespoon icing sugar

Whipped cream

---

1 Preheat oven to 170°C/325°F/gas 3. Grease and flour 23 cm/9 inch springform cake tin.

2 In heavy non-stick saucepan over low heat, heat plain chocolate and butter, stirring often, until melted and smooth. Remove pan from heat.

3 In large bowl, with electric mixer on full speed, beat egg whites until soft peaks form; gradually sprinkle in 60 g/2 oz caster sugar, beating until sugar completely dissolves and whites stand in stiff peaks.

4 In another large bowl, using electric mixer, beat egg yolks and remaining caster sugar until very thick and lemon-coloured, about 5 minutes. Add melted chocolate mixture, beating until well mixed.

5 Add flour to mixture; continue beating until blended, occasionally scraping bowl with rubber spatula.

6 With rubber spatula or wire whisk, gently fold beaten egg whites into chocolate mixture, one-third at a time.

7 Spoon mixture into tin, spreading evenly. Bake for 30-35 minutes (cake will rise and crack on top while baking).

8 Cake is done when mixture appears set and when skewer inserted in centre comes out moist (but centre should not be runny).

9 Cool cake completely in tin on wire rack (cake will fall and top will crack as it cools).

10 Meanwhile, using plain chocolate flavour cake covering, make Chocolate Curls (page 58).

11 With palette knife, loosen cake from side of tin; remove tin side. Place cake on serving plate.

Icing sugar can be sifted over cake as liberally as you like

TO SERVE
Sift icing sugar over top of cake; decorate with chocolate curls. Serve with whipped cream.

Cracks on top of cake are unavoidable, and quite acceptable with this type of very rich continental-style chocolate cake. No-one will notice once they have taken their first ecstatic bite

CHOCOLATE CARAQUE CAKE

The long, thin scrolls on this spectacular chocolate cake are called 'caraque' in French cooking. In this recipe they are made with chocolate cake covering, which is very easy to use.

CHOCOLATE GLAZE
In small heavy saucepan over very low heat, heat *90 g/3 oz plain chocolate, broken into pieces, 45 g/1 ¹/₂ oz butter* and *2 teaspoons golden syrup*, stirring frequently, until melted and smooth. Remove from heat; stir frequently until glaze cools and thickens slightly.

  8 servings
Can be made day before and kept in a cool place

150 g/5 oz self-raising flour

150 g/5 oz caster sugar

175 ml/6 fl oz soured cream

120 g/4 oz butter, softened

30 g/1 oz cocoa powder

¹/₂ teaspoon baking powder

1 egg

175 g/6 oz plain chocolate flavour cake covering

Chocolate Glaze (see Box, above right)

Icing sugar for sifting

1 Grease 23 cm/9 inch round cake tin; line bottom of tin with non-stick baking parchment.

2 Preheat oven to 180°C/350°F/gas 4. In large bowl, with electric mixer, beat first 7 ingredients until blended, occasionally scraping bowl.

3 Spread mixture evenly in tin. Bake for about 30-35 minutes or until skewer inserted in centre comes out clean. Cool in tin on wire rack for 10 minutes. With palette knife, loosen cake from edge of tin; turn out on to wire rack; peel off parchment. Cool completely.

4 Meanwhile, in small bowl over pan of gently simmering water, heat chocolate, stirring often, until melted and smooth. Pour on to 2 large baking sheets, spread evenly and make Chocolate Scrolls (see Box, below).

5 Make more Chocolate Scrolls with chocolate cake covering on second baking sheet. (Consistency of cake covering is very important. If it is too soft, it will not curl; if too hard, it will crumble. If too firm, leave it to stand at room temperature for a few minutes until soft enough to work with; if too soft, return to refrigerator.) Refrigerate scrolls until firm.

6 Make Chocolate Glaze.

7 Carefully brush away crumbs from cake. Place cake on wire rack over greaseproof paper.

8 Spoon Chocolate Glaze over top and side of cake (some glaze will drip on to greaseproof paper underneath).

9 Leave cake to stand at room temperature until glaze is firm, about 45 minutes.

10 Transfer cake to plate. Arrange Chocolate Scrolls on top and sift over icing sugar.

CHOCOLATE SCROLLS

Spreading chocolate: with palette knife, spread melted chocolate flavour cake covering over baking sheets to cover evenly. Refrigerate until firm but not brittle, about 10 minutes.

Making scrolls: place 1 chocolate-covered baking sheet on damp cloth on work surface (damp cloth keeps baking sheet from moving while working). Using straight-edged knife or palette knife, push blade across chocolate to form long, thin scrolls.

Transferring scrolls: with cocktail stick, transfer scrolls to another baking sheet.

CHOCOLATE TRUFFLE CAKE

A gâteau for a special occasion, Chocolate Truffle Cake is a deep, three-layer cake filled and piped with a wickedly rich chocolate truffle mixture. The satiny smooth glaze, a luscious combination of cream and chocolate, gives the finished cake a professional look, yet it is remarkably simple to do.

10 servings
Can be made day before and kept in refrigerator

650 g/1 lb 6 oz plain chocolate, broken into pieces

250 g/9 oz unsalted butter, softened

3 eggs, separated

175 g/6 oz caster sugar

250 g/9 oz self-raising flour

300 g/10 oz icing sugar, sifted

175 ml/6 fl oz double or whipping cream

Rose to decorate

1 Grease and base line a 23 cm/9 inch round springform cake tin. Preheat oven to 170°C/325°F/gas 3.

2 In a medium saucepan over low heat, melt 250 g/9 oz chocolate, 175 g/6 oz butter and *100 ml/3 fl oz water*, stirring frequently, until smooth. Remove from the heat and cool.

3 In large bowl, whisk the egg yolks and caster sugar together until thick and pale. Gradually whisk in the chocolate mixture until smooth.

4 Sift the flour over the chocolate mixture and fold in using a spatula until evenly blended. Using clean beaters, whisk the egg whites until stiff. Fold into the cake mixture until the egg whites have been incorporated.

5 Pour into tin. Bake for 75-85 minutes or until a skewer inserted in centre of cake comes out clean. Cool cake for 10 minutes, turn out, remove paper and cool on a wire rack. When cold, cut into 3 even layers.

6 Meanwhile, prepare truffle mixture: in bowl over pan of gently simmering water, heat 120 g/4 oz chocolate, stirring frequently, until melted; cool slightly. Stir in icing sugar, remaining butter and 4 tablespoons double or whipping cream until mixture is smooth and well blended.

7 Prepare glaze: in heavy medium saucepan over low heat, heat 225 g/8 oz chocolate and remaining double or whipping cream, stirring frequently, until melted, smooth and slightly thickened; keep warm.

8 Assemble and glaze cake (see Box, below). Refrigerate cake until glaze is set, about 30 minutes.

9 Remove cake to plate. Pipe border with remaining truffle mixture (see Box, below). Grate remaining chocolate; sprinkle round top edge of cake. Place rose in centre.

ASSEMBLING, GLAZING AND DECORATING CAKE

Assembling cake: *with palette knife, spread 1 cake layer with about one-sixth of truffle mixture. Top with second cake layer, pressing down gently but firmly. Spread with another one-sixth of truffle mixture; top with third cake layer.*

Glazing cake: *over assembled cake, pour prepared glaze. With palette knife, spread glaze to cover top and side of cake completely.*

Piping border: *with star tube, pipe border of remaining truffle mixture round bottom of cake.*

GRANNY'S CAKE

8 servings
Can be made day
before

400 g/14 oz caster sugar

225 g/8 oz butter, softened

350 g/12 oz self-raising
flour

250 ml/8 fl oz milk

1/2 teaspoon baking powder

4 eggs

Icing sugar for sprinkling

Cherries to decorate
(optional)

1 Preheat oven to
180°C/350°F/gas 4.
Lightly grease and flour
23 cm/9 inch fluted
kugelhopf mould or
savarin mould.

2 In large bowl, with
electric mixer, beat
caster sugar and butter
for 10 minutes or until
light and fluffy, scraping
bowl frequently with
rubber spatula.

3 Add flour, milk,
baking powder and
eggs; beat ingredients until
well mixed, constantly
scraping bowl.

4 Beat mixture for a
further 2 minutes,
occasionally scraping bowl.

5 Spread mixture evenly
in mould.

6 Bake cake in oven for
50-55 minutes or until
skewer inserted in centre
comes out clean. Cool
cake in mould on wire
rack for 10 minutes, then
turn out on to wire rack to
cool completely.

7 Sift icing sugar
over cake.

*A pretty doiley sets off this cake
a treat, especially when the
colours tone so well with the
serving plate and cherry
decoration*

*A liberal
sprinkling of
icing sugar
adds an
attractive
decorative
touch to a
plain and
simple cake*

TO SERVE
*If you like, decorate side of
cake with cherries.*

ALMOND SCALLOP CAKES

Makes 8
Allow 2 hours preparation and cooking time

150 g/5 oz blanched
  almonds

215 g/7 ½ oz self-raising
  flour

200 g/7 oz caster sugar

2 eggs

150 ml/ ¼ pint milk

2 tablespoons vegetable oil

1 teaspoon almond essence

Strawberries to decorate

1 In small frying pan over medium heat, cook blanched almonds until golden, stirring often; cool. In food processor or blender, finely grind toasted almonds. (If using blender, grind nuts in 2 batches.)

2 Preheat oven to 180°C/350°F/gas 4. Generously grease eight 12.5 cm/5 inch or 125 ml/ 4 fl oz scallop shell-shaped moulds.

These pretty little teacakes are flecked with ground toasted almonds; if you prefer, you can use walnuts or pecans instead

3 In large bowl, mix ground almonds, flour and sugar.

4 In small bowl, beat eggs lightly; stir in next 3 ingredients.

Spooning mixture into shell moulds

Golden-brown edges add to the visual appeal of the dainty scallop shapes

5 Stir liquid mixture into flour mixture just until flour is moistened. Spoon mixture evenly into moulds, leaving 1 cm/ ½ inch border all round moulds.

6 To keep moulds level while baking, arrange them on top of 2 large bun tins, or arrange them on crumpled pieces of foil in baking tray.

7 Bake cakes in oven for 20-25 minutes or until skewer inserted in centres comes out clean.

8 Cool cakes in moulds on wire racks for 5 minutes. Run tip of knife round edges of moulds to loosen cakes; turn cakes out on to wire racks to cool completely. Serve with strawberries.

DECORATING WITH CHOCOLATE

A chocolate butterfly perched on top of a simple dessert will delight the sophisticated dinner party guest as much as it will enchant children at a birthday party. Like the majority of chocolate decorations, butterflies require no special skill, but they do need time for the chocolate to harden. All chocolate decorations except curls can be made with real chocolate; for making curls, use plain chocolate flavour cake covering, which is more manageable.

To melt chocolate: break it into pieces and place in a small bowl over a pan of gently simmering water. Heat for about 5 minutes or until melted and smooth, stirring often with rubber spatula. If using for piping, leave to cool first.

NON-TOXIC LEAVES
These non-toxic leaves are safe for making chocolate leaves: gardenia, grape, lemon, magnolia, nasturtium, rose, violet.

Do not use the following leaves in contact with chocolate or other foods: amaryllis, azalea, caladium, daffodil, delphinium, dieffenbachia, English ivy, hydrangea, jonquil, larkspur, laurel, lily of the valley, mistletoe, narcissus, oleander, poinsettia, rhododendron.

Wash non-toxic leaves in warm, soapy water; rinse and dry well before use.

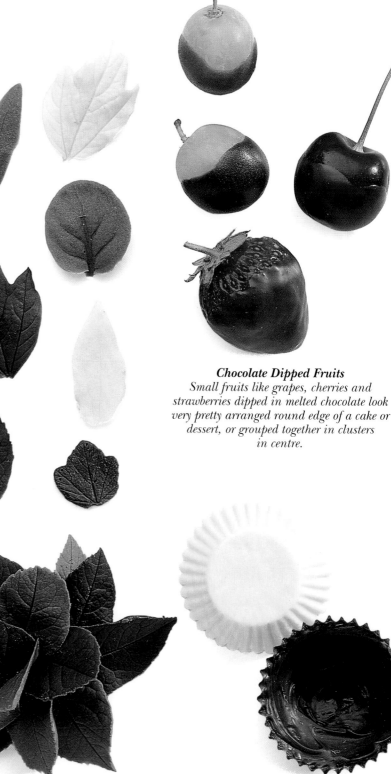

Chocolate Dipped Fruits
Small fruits like grapes, cherries and strawberries dipped in melted chocolate look very pretty arranged round edge of a cake or dessert, or grouped together in clusters in centre.

Chocolate Leaves
A variety of leaves is brushed with different kinds of melted chocolate to make interesting shapes and colours. Grouping chocolate leaves together in centre of dessert or cake to make a flower shape is especially effective.

Chocolate Cups
Miniature paper or foil cake cases are used as moulds for melted chocolate, then peeled off when chocolate is firm. Filled with piped whipped cream, icing or pieces of fruit, they look good on the edge of plates and platters.

Lacy Lattice
Melted chocolate piped free-hand in lattice design on non-stick baking parchment is refrigerated until firm, then carefully lifted off.

Chocolate Heart
Heart shape is cut out of melted and chilled plain chocolate with a biscuit cutter, then piped with melted white chocolate. Hole is punched with fine skewer for ribbon to be threaded through.

Chocolate Scrolls
Elegant curls are made by pushing knife or palette knife across surface of melted and cooled plain chocolate flavour cake covering.

Chocolate Ruffles
These are made like Chocolate Scrolls (left), but knife or palette knife is pushed only halfway across surface of melted and cooled plain chocolate flavour cake covering.

Dainty Daisy
Melted plain chocolate is piped over daisy design on non-stick baking parchment, then left to set before being flooded with melted white chocolate. Daisy is refrigerated until firm, then lifted off parchment.

Simple Curls
These can be made quickly by warming bar of milky white chocolate or plain chocolate flavour cake covering in your hands, then drawing a vegetable peeler along it to produce short, plump shapes.

Fleur-de-Lis
Shape of fleur-de-lis is drawn on non-stick baking parchment, then melted chocolate piped over. Decoration is refrigerated until firm before being carefully lifted off and placed on dessert.

Marbled Triangles
Melted plain and white chocolates are swirled together to make marbled design, then refrigerated until firm. Triangles are then stamped out with small cutter.

CHOCOLATE DIPPED FRUIT

Cherries dipped in melted plain and white chocolates

1 Rinse fruit under cold running water but do not remove stalks; pat completely dry with kitchen paper; set fruit aside. (For dipping, fruit should be at room temperature.)

2 Melt chocolate in small bowl over pan of gently simmering water (page 56); leave to cool slightly.

3 With fingers, hold stalk of 1 fruit at a time and dip it into chocolate, leaving part of fruit uncovered.

4 Shake off excess chocolate; place fruit on non-stick baking parchment. Leave to stand until chocolate is set, about 10 minutes; remove from parchment.

CHOCOLATE CURLS

Chocolate Scrolls (see Box, page 50), together with white Chocolate Curls

1 Hold bar or piece of milky white or Swiss white chocolate or plain chocolate flavour cake covering between palms of hands to soften chocolate slightly.

2 Slowly and firmly draw blade of vegetable peeler across wide side of chocolate for wide curls, thin side for thin curls.

3 Use cocktail stick to transfer curls, to avoid breaking them.

CHOCOLATE BUTTERFLIES

Two-Tone Butterfly made with piped melted plain and white chocolates

1 With pencil, draw butterflies on rectangles of baking parchment. Place rectangles on clean flat surface, pencil-side down; tape to work surface.

2 Spoon melted plain chocolate (page 56) into paper piping bag with tip cut to make 3 mm/⅛ inch hole (or small piping bag with small writing tube).

3 Pipe melted plain chocolate on to non-stick baking parchment rectangle in thin continuous lines over butterfly outline. Refrigerate until set.

4 Spoon melted white chocolate into clean paper piping bag; pipe inside outline. Refrigerate until firm, 1 hour.

CHOCOLATE TRIANGLES

Plain and white chocolate triangles

CHOCOLATE SQUIGGLES

Plain chocolate squiggles

CHOCOLATE LEAVES

Chocolate leaves in different colours and shapes

1 Tape sheet of non-stick baking parchment to clean work surface.

2 With palette knife, spread melted chocolate (page 56) on sheet of non-stick baking parchment. Refrigerate until chocolate is set.

3 With small decorative cutter, cut out chocolate shapes. Refrigerate shapes until firm.

1 Spoon melted chocolate (page 56) into paper piping bag with tip cut to 3 mm/ ¹/₈ inch hole .

2 On to non-stick baking parchment rectangles, pipe melted chocolate in free-hand squiggle designs.

3 Refrigerate chocolate squiggles until they are firm.

4 With palette knife, carefully lift chocolate squiggles off baking parchment.

1 Rinse leaves of your choice (see Box, page 56); pat dry with kitchen paper.

2 With pastry brush, small painting brush or small palette knife, spread layer of melted chocolate (page 56) on underside of leaves (using underside will give a more distinctive leaf design).

3 Refrigerate chocolate-coated leaves until chocolate is firm, about 30 minutes.

4 With cool hands, carefully peel leaves away from chocolate.

HAZELNUT AND CREAM SWISS ROLL

12 servings
Can be made day
before and kept in
refrigerator

4 eggs, separated

120 g/4 oz icing sugar
plus extra for sprinkling

120 g/4 oz self-raising
flour

300 ml/ 1/2 pint double
cream

120 g/4 oz hazelnut kernels

1 tablespoon liquid honey

1 Grease 33 x 23 cm/
13 x 9 inch Swiss roll
tin; line tin with non-stick
baking parchment.

2 In large bowl, with
electric mixer on full
speed, beat egg whites
until soft peaks form;
gradually sift in 60 g/2 oz
icing sugar, beating until
sugar completely dissolves
and whites stand in
stiff peaks.

3 Preheat oven to
190°C/375°F/gas 5.

4 In another large bowl,
using electric mixer,
beat egg yolks and 60 g/
2 oz sifted icing sugar until
very thick and lemon-
coloured. Add flour;
beat until well mixed,
constantly scraping bowl
with rubber spatula.

5 With rubber spatula
or wire whisk, gently
fold beaten egg whites
into egg yolk mixture,
one-third at a time.

6 Spoon mixture into
tin, spreading evenly.
Bake for 12-15 minutes or
until cake springs back
when lightly touched with
finger.

MAKING SWISS ROLL

1 Sift icing sugar over
clean tea towel. When
cake is done, immedi-
ately turn out on to
towel.

2 With fingers, carefully
peel non-stick baking
parchment off cake. If you
like, cut off crisp edges.

3 Starting at a narrow
end, roll cake with towel.
Place roll, seam-side
down, on wire rack; leave
to cool completely.

7 Make Swiss roll (see
Box, above).

8 While Swiss roll is
cooling, whip double
cream until stiff peaks
form.

9 In small frying pan
over medium heat,
cook hazelnuts until
golden, stirring
frequently; cool.

10 Coarsely chop
12 toasted hazel-
nuts and reserve for
decoration; finely chop
remaining toasted hazel-
nuts to use in filling.

11 Fold finely
chopped hazelnuts
and honey into half of the
whipped double cream.

12 Unroll cooled
Swiss roll; spread
top of cake evenly with
whipped cream, honey
and hazelnut mixture.

13 Starting at same
narrow end, roll
cake without towel and
then place on platter.

ALTERNATIVE FILLING

The whipped cream, hazelnut and honey filling in
the main recipe on this page is very quick and easy to
do. If you have more time and would like a richer
flavour, try the following Maple Cream Filling.

Maple Cream Filling
In medium saucepan,
place *2 tablespoons plain
flour*; with wire whisk or
spoon, slowly stir in
150 ml/ 1/4 pint milk and
5 tablespoons maple syrup
until smooth.
   Cook over medium
heat, stirring constantly,
until mixture boils; boil
for 1 minute until thick.
Remove saucepan from
heat.
   In cup, with fork, beat
2 egg yolks lightly; stir in
small amount of hot
maple mixture. Slowly
pour egg mixture back
into remaining maple
mixture in pan, stirring
rapidly with spoon to
prevent lumping; cook
over low heat, stirring
constantly, until mixture
thickens and coats back
of spoon well, about
5 minutes (do not boil or
mixture may curdle).
   Remove saucepan from
heat and pour filling into
bowl. To keep skin from
forming on top of filling
as it cools, press a sheet of
dampened greaseproof
paper directly on to
surface of hot filling.

14 Spoon remaining
whipped cream
into piping bag with large
star tube; pipe whipped
cream on Swiss roll to
make attractive design.
Refrigerate roll if not
serving immediately.

TO SERVE
Just before serving,
sprinkle reserved coarsely
chopped hazelnuts over
whipped cream on
top of cake.

CELEBRATION BUFFET CAKE

🍴 8-10 servings
🕐 Can be made day before and kept in refrigerator

450 g/1 lb plain chocolate, broken into pieces
350 ml/12 fl oz double or whipping cream
125 ml/4 fl oz cream liqueur
2 x 225 g/8 oz packets sponge cake mix
30 g/1 oz cocoa powder
Strawberries to decorate

1 Place chocolate in large bowl. In medium saucepan over medium heat, heat double or whipping cream and cream liqueur until tiny bubbles form round edge of pan; pour hot cream mixture into bowl with chocolate. With electric mixer, beat until chocolate melts and mixture is smooth. Cover and refrigerate chocolate ganache until thickened.

2 Preheat oven to 180°C/350°F/gas 4. Line two 33 x 23 cm/ 13 x 9 inch Swiss roll tins with non-stick baking parchment.

3 Prepare sponge mixture according to packet instructions. Spoon half of the mixture into 1 Swiss roll tin and spread evenly. Sift three-quarters of the cocoa into remaining mixture; stir well. Spread in second tin.

4 Bake cakes for 10 minutes or until skewer inserted in centre comes out clean. Cool in tins on wire racks for 10 minutes. With palette knife, loosen cakes; turn out on to wire racks, peel off parchment and cool.

5 With serrated knife, using cardboard strip as guide, cut each cake in half lengthways, to make 4 equal strips in all.

6 With electric mixer, beat chilled chocolate ganache until thick and with an easy spreading consistency.

7 Place 1 white cake strip on large baking sheet; spread with 5 tablespoons chocolate ganache. Top with 1 chocolate cake strip; spread with 5 tablespoons chocolate ganache.

8 Repeat layering, ending with chocolate cake strip. Set aside remaining ganache.

9 Cover cake and place in freezer until chocolate ganache filling is firm, about 1 hour.

10 Assemble and ice cake (see Box, right). Sift remaining cocoa powder over cake.

11 Transfer cake to serving plate; refrigerate if not serving immediately.

12 To serve, decorate cake with whole fresh strawberries.

ASSEMBLING CAKE

Cutting cake diagonally: place frozen cake on work surface with long side parallel to edge. With long serrated knife, slice cake in half diagonally from upper rear corner to lower front corner, to make 2 long triangles. Place 1 cake half on foil-covered cardboard strip, cut side facing out.

Spreading first cake half with chocolate ganache: on uncut side of cake half on foil-covered cardboard strip, with palette knife, evenly spread 5 tablespoons chocolate ganache.

Joining cake halves: place second cake half, cut side facing outwards, alongside first cake half. Gently press 2 halves together to form 1 large triangle.

Icing cake: spread sloping sides of triangle cake with remaining chocolate ganache.

No-one will believe that this dramatic-looking triangle cake is quick and easy to make – with a sponge mix from a packet!

SWEET PIES

Sweet pies can be as simple and homely or as elaborate and elegant as you wish. Much of their success depends on the pastry, which should enhance, not compete with, the flavour of the filling and be crisp and tender, never soggy. For variety, try a plain top crust one time, a lattice top the next. For biscuit crust pies, try different fillings and toppings. Be creative!

SHORTCRUST PASTRY FOR DOUBLE CRUST PIE

| 300 g/10 oz plain flour |
| 1 teaspoon salt (optional) |
| 175 g/6 oz butter or block margarine |
| 3-4 tablespoons cold water |

1 Make dough as for Shortcrust Pastry for Pie Shell (see Box, right), steps 1 to 3.

2 Divide dough into 2 pieces, 1 slightly larger than the other.

3 On lightly floured surface, with floured rolling pin, roll out larger piece of dough into round about 3 mm/ 1/8 inch thick and 4 cm/1 1/2 inches larger all round than upside-down shallow 20-23 cm/8-9 inch pie dish.

4 Roll dough round gently on to rolling pin; transfer to pie dish and unroll. Gently ease dough into bottom and up side of pie dish to line evenly; trim dough edge and fill according to individual recipe instructions.

5 For top crust, roll out smaller piece of dough as for bottom crust; with sharp knife, cut few slashes or design in centre of round; centre top crust over filling in bottom crust.

6 Make Decorative Pastry Edge (pages 66-67); bake pie according to recipe.

MAKING PASTRY IN FOOD PROCESSOR

To save time, pastry dough can be made in the food processor, with excellent results. This is especially helpful if you are catering for a crowd and have a large number of pies to make.

1 In food processor with knife blade attached, combine flour and butter or margarine. Process for 1-2 seconds until mixture forms fine crumbs.

2 Add cold water; process for 1-2 seconds until dough forms on blades.

3 Remove dough from bowl; with hands, shape dough into ball.

SHORTCRUST PASTRY FOR PIE SHELL

| 200 g/7 oz plain flour |
| 1 teaspoon salt (optional) |
| 120 g/4 oz butter or block margarine |
| 2-3 tablespoons cold water |

1 In medium bowl, stir flour and salt, if using.

2 With pastry blender or with fingertips, cut or rub butter or margarine into flour mixture until mixture resembles coarse crumbs.

3 Sprinkle cold water, a tablespoon at a time, into mixture. Mix lightly with fork after each addition, until dough is just moist enough to hold together.

8 Roll dough round gently on to rolling pin; transfer to pie dish and unroll.

4 In same bowl, with lightly floured hands, shape dough into smooth ball.

5 On floured surface, with floured rolling pin, roll out dough into round about 3 mm/ 1/8 inch thick.

9 Gently ease dough into bottom and up side of pie dish to line evenly.

10 Make Decorative Pastry Edge (pages 66-67); fill and bake pie according to recipe.

6 Roll from centre to edge of dough to keep dough circular. Add more flour if dough begins to stick to work surface. Push sides in by hand if necessary and lift rolling pin slightly near edges to avoid making them too thin.

7 Cut dough round 4 cm/1 1/2 inches larger all round than upside-down 20-23 cm/ 8-9 inch pie dish.

BAKING BLIND

Many pie shells are filled with an uncooked mixture, so you will need to bake the pie shell blind first. A crisp baked pastry shell that is to be filled with a chilled mixture should be thoroughly cooled before the filling is added.

1 Preheat oven to 220°C/425°F/gas 7. Line dish with dough.

2 With fork, prick dough liberally.

3 Line dough with foil and spread evenly with dried or baking beans.

4 Bake for 15 minutes or until golden.

5 Remove foil and beans, prick again and bake for a further 3-4 minutes.

6 Cool on wire rack.

DECORATIVE PASTRY EDGES

These eye-catching edges that finish off a pie so beautifully are not hard to make. Choose from Fluted, Sharp Fluted and Ruffled Edges for either pie shells or double crust pies; Leaf, Plaited and Heart Edges are suitable for pie shells only.

Pie Shells

1 Line pie dish with dough (page 65); trim dough edge with kitchen scissors, leaving about 2.5 cm/1 inch overhang all round rim of dish.

2 Fold overhang under, then bring up over rim of pie dish.

3 Make decorative edge of your choice, then bake pie as directed in recipe.

Double Crust Pies

1 Trim edge of top crust with kitchen scissors, leaving about 2.5 cm/1 inch overhang all round rim of pie dish. Fold overhang under, then bring up over rim of pie dish.

2 Make decorative edge of your choice, then bake pie as directed in recipe.

FLUTED EDGE

1 *Pinch to form stand-up edge. Place index finger on inside edge of dough and, with index finger and thumb of other hand, pinch dough to make flute.*

2 *Repeat round edge of dough, leaving 5 mm/¼ inch space between each flute.*

SHARP FLUTED EDGE

1 *Pinch to form stand-up edge. Place pointed edge of small star or diamond shaped biscuit cutter on inside edge of dough and, with index finger and thumb of other hand, pinch dough to make sharp flute.*

2 *Repeat round edge of dough, leaving 5 mm/¼ inch space between each flute.*

LEAF OR HEART EDGE   RUFFLED EDGE   PLAITED EDGE

1 *Prepare Shortcrust Pastry for Double Crust Pie (page 64); use larger piece of dough to line pie dish.*

2 *Roll out remaining dough until it is 3 mm/ 1/8 inch thick. With sharp knife or small biscuit cutter, cut out shapes (leaves or hearts).*

3 *Press each shape on to lightly moistened pie shell edge, overlapping shapes slightly or varying angles.*

1 *Pinch to form stand-up edge. Place index finger under outside edge of dough and, with index finger and thumb of other hand, pinch dough to form ruffle.*

2 *Repeat round edge of dough, leaving 5 mm/ 1/4 inch space between ruffles.*

1 *Prepare Shortcrust Pastry for Double Crust Pie (page 64); use larger piece of dough to line pie dish.*

2 *Roll out remaining dough until it is about 3 mm/ 1/8 inch thick; cut into strips that are 5 mm/ 1/4 inch wide.*

3 *Gently plait strips together and press on to lightly moistened pie shell edge. Join ends of plait together to cover edge completely.*

HARVEST PEAR AND PINEAPPLE PIE

10 servings

Allow 2 hours preparation and cooking time

Filling

2 x 820 g/29 oz cans pear halves

2 x 400 g/14 oz cans pineapple pieces in juice

1 rounded tablespoon cornflour

1/2 teaspoon grated nutmeg

1/2 teaspoon ground cinnamon

45 g/1 1/2 oz butter

Pastry

225 g/8 oz plain flour

1/2 teaspoon salt (optional)

120 g/4 oz butter or block margarine

1 egg yolk, lightly beaten

Good for a crowd, this fruit pie is given a neat, professional finish with a Rope Edge

1 Drain pears, reserving 400 ml/14 fl oz juice; thinly slice pear halves. Drain pineapple.

2 In large saucepan, mix cornflour, nutmeg, cinnamon and reserved pear juice. Cook over medium heat, stirring constantly, until mixture thickens and boils. Remove saucepan from heat; stir in pear slices and pineapple pieces.

3 Into 23 cm/9 inch square baking dish, pour fruit mixture.

Pouring fruit mixture into baking dish

4 Cut butter into into small pieces; dot over fruit. Leave filling to cool to room temperature, about 30 minutes.

5 Meanwhile, prepare pastry dough: in bowl, mix flour with salt, if using. With pastry blender or with fingertips, cut or rub butter or margarine into flour until mixture resembles coarse crumbs. Sprinkle *3 tablespoons cold water*, a tablespoon at a time, into mixture, mixing lightly with fork after each addition until dough is moist enough to hold together. Shape dough into a ball.

6 Preheat oven to 220°C/425°F/gas 7. On floured surface, with floured rolling pin, roll out dough 3 mm/1/8 inch thick to fit dish, leaving 2.5 cm/1 inch overhang; place over filling.

7 Turn overhang under to make stand-up edge. Make Rope Edge (see Box, right).

8 Cut a few slashes in crust to allow steam to escape during baking. Brush crust lightly with egg yolk.

9 Bake pie for 25-30 minutes until filling is bubbly and pastry is golden brown. Cool pie on wire rack for 15 minutes before serving, or cool completely to serve cold later.

ROPE EDGE

Press thumb into edge of crust at an angle, then pinch dough between thumb and knuckle of index finger. Place thumb in groove that has been left by index finger.

Repeat all round edge of crust to create twisted rope effect.

BLUEBERRY PIE

10 servings
Allow 3 hours preparation and cooking time

Pastry

300 g/10 oz plain flour
³/₄ teaspoon salt (optional)
175 g/6 oz butter or block margarine
1 egg
2 teaspoons caster sugar

Filling

700 g/1 ¹/₂ lb fresh or frozen (thawed) blueberries
100 g/3 ¹/₂ oz caster sugar
1 teaspoon grated lemon zest
15 g/ ¹/₂ oz butter

1 First prepare pastry dough: in large bowl, with fork, stir flour with salt, if using. With pastry blender or fingertips, cut or rub butter or margarine into flour mixture until mixture resembles coarse crumbs. In cup, beat egg lightly. Add egg to flour mixture, mixing lightly with fork until dough will hold together, adding a little *cold water* if necessary. With hands, shape dough into 2 balls, 1 slightly larger than the other.

2 On lightly floured surface, with floured rolling pin, roll out larger ball of dough into round about 4 cm/1 ¹/₂ inches larger all round than upside-down shallow 20-23 cm/8-9 inch pie dish. Ease dough into pie dish to line evenly.

3 If using frozen blueberries, they should be drained. In large bowl, with rubber spatula, gently toss blueberries with caster sugar and grated lemon zest.

4 Spoon blueberry mixture into pie shell. Cut butter into small pieces; dot on top of blueberry mixture.

5 Preheat oven to 220°C/425°F/gas 7. Roll out remaining dough as before. Moisten edge of pie shell with water; place top crust over filling.

6 Trim dough edge, leaving about 4 cm/1 ¹/₂ inch overhang. Fold overhang under; make Sharp Fluted or other Decorative Pastry Edge (pages 66-67).

7 With sharp knife, cut 10 cm/4 inch 'X' in centre of top crust.

8 Fold back points of 'X' to make square opening in centre of pie.

9 Sprinkle top of pie with 2 teaspoons caster sugar.

10 Bake pie for 40 minutes or until filling begins to bubble and pastry is golden. If pastry browns too quickly, cover edge loosely with foil. Cool pie on wire rack before serving. Serve warm or cold.

STRAWBERRY AND RHUBARB PIE

Strawberries and rhubarb go together really well, both in terms of colour and flavour – and they're in season at the same time, making them the perfect combination for this lucious-tasting pie.

8-10 servings
Allow 3 hours preparation and cooking time

Filling

450 g/1 lb strawberries	
450 g/1 lb rhubarb (trimmed weight)	
175 g/6 oz caster sugar	
45 g/1½ oz plain flour	
15 g/½ oz butter	

Pastry

Shortcrust Pastry for Double Crust Pie (page 64)
1 tablespoon milk

1 Remove hulls from strawberries and cut each strawberry in half. Cut rhubarb stalks crossways into 1 cm/½ inch-thick pieces.

2 In large bowl, with rubber spatula, gently toss halved strawberries, rhubarb pieces, sugar and flour.

3 Prepare pastry dough.

4 On lightly floured surface, with floured rolling pin, roll out two-two-thirds of dough into 40 cm/16 inch round.

5 Gently ease dough into bottom and up side of 20-23 cm/8-9 inch pie dish that is at least 4 cm/1 ½ inches deep, to line evenly; trim dough edge, leaving 4 cm/1 ½ inch overhang.

6 Into pie shell, spoon strawberry and rhubarb mixture.

7 Cut butter into small pieces and dot evenly over strawberry and rhubarb mixture.

8 Preheat oven to 220°C/425°F/gas 7.

9 Roll out remaining dough into a 26.5cm/10 ½ inch round. With fluted pastry wheel or knife, cut into ten 2 cm/³/4 inch wide strips.

10 Place 5 strips over filling; do not seal ends.

11 With remaining 5 strips, make Diamond Lattice (see Box, page 71).

12 Trim ends of strips; moisten edge of pie shell with water; press ends of strips to pie shell to seal. Bring overhang up over strips; pinch edges to seal; make Ruffled or other Decorative Pastry Edge (pages 66-67). Brush lattice with milk.

13 Bake pie for 45-50 minutes or until fruit mixture bubbles and pastry is golden. After 30 minutes, cover pie loosely with foil if pastry is browning too quickly.

14 Leave pie to stand for 1 hour to allow juices to set slightly; serve warm or cold.

Tossing strawberry and rhubarb mixture

ALTERNATIVE TO LATTICE

A quick-and-easy alternative pastry topping to the Diamond Lattice in the main picture (page 71) is this Cartwheel, in which the pastry strips are placed over the filling like the spokes of a wheel.

Cartwheel

1 With fluted pastry wheel or knife, cut dough into twelve 1 cm/ ½-inch strips.

2 Arrange 6 strips over filling in 'V' shapes.

3 Use more strips to make smaller 'V' shapes inside larger ones.

4 If you like, cut out small shapes from dough trimmings and place in centre of pie.

DIAMOND LATTICE

Taking pastry strips back: *fold back every other strip three-quarters of its length.*

Placing second cross strip: *arrange another cross strip, parallel to central strip, 2.5 cm/1 inch away.*

Placing central cross strip: *arrange 1 strip diagonally across centre of filling to start forming diamond shape, then take folded part of strips over central strip.*

Folding back alternate strips: *fold back strips that were not folded back before.*

Replacing folded part of strips: *take folded part of strips over second diagonal cross strip. Continue folding back alternate strips and placing cross strips diagonally across filling to weave diamond pattern.*

Crinkled edges on pastry lattice are made by cutting out strips with a pastry wheel

Luscious filling of fresh strawberries and rhubarb can be seen through 'windows' of diamond lattice

LEMON MERINGUE PIE

6-8 servings
Allow 50 minutes
preparation and
cooking time

Crumb Crust

175 g/6 oz digestive
    biscuits

75 g/2 ½ oz butter

45 g/1 ½ oz demerara
    sugar

Lemon Filling

Grated zest and juice of
    2 large lemons

45 g/1 ½ oz cornflour

2 egg yolks

75 g/2 ½ oz caster sugar

Topping

3 egg whites

120 g/4 oz caster sugar

*Meringue topping
is swirled over
lemon filling, but it
can be piped for a
more formal effect*

1 Make crumb crust: place digestive biscuits in polythene bag; with rolling pin, roll biscuits into fine crumbs.

2 Melt butter in small saucepan over gentle heat, add sugar and biscuit crumbs and mix well.

3 Turn biscuit mixture into deepish 23 cm/ 9 inch flan dish; with back of metal spoon, press mixture on to bottom and up side of dish.

Pressing crushed biscuit mixture on to bottom and up side of flan dish

4 Make lemon filling: put lemon zest and juice in bowl with cornflour; blend to a smooth paste.

5 In medium saucepan, bring *300 ml/ ½ pint water* to the boil; pour on to cornflour mixture. Return cornflour mixture to pan, bring to the boil and simmer for 3 minutes until thick, stirring.

6 Remove saucepan from heat; add egg yolks and caster sugar. Return to heat; cook for 1 minute, to thicken sauce. Cool slightly, then spoon into biscuit crust.

7 Preheat oven to 170°C/325°F/ gas 3.

8 Make topping: in large bowl, with electric mixer on full speed, beat egg whites until soft peaks form. Add caster sugar, 1 tablespoon at a time, beating well after each addition until sugar dissolves completely and egg whites stand in stiff, glossy peaks.

9 Spoon topping over lemon filling, taking care to spread it right to edge of crust, leaving no spaces.

10 Bake pie for about 30 minutes or until meringue is golden brown. Serve warm or cold.

OLD ENGLISH APPLE PIE

🍴 8 servings
🕐 Allow 2 hours preparation and cooking time

Filling

8 medium-sized Bramley apples

2 teaspoons lemon juice

1 tablespoon cornflour

100 g/3 ½ oz caster sugar

15 g/ ½ oz butter

Pastry

Shortcrust Pastry for Double Crust Pie (page 64)

Milk for glazing

1 tablespoon caster sugar

7 slices processed cheese (optional)

1 Peel and core apples; cut into thin slices. In large bowl, with rubber spatula, lightly toss apple slices, lemon juice, cornflour and sugar; set aside.

2 Prepare pastry dough. Divide into 2 pieces, 1 slightly larger. On lightly floured surface, with floured rolling pin, roll out larger piece of dough into round about 4 cm/ 1 ½ inches larger all round than upside-down shallow 20-23 cm/8-9 inch pie dish. Ease dough into pie dish to line evenly; trim dough edge, leaving 2.5 cm/1 inch overhang. Reserve dough trimmings.

Pastry crust is sprinkled with sugar before baking to give finished pie a frosted top

3 Spoon apple mixture into pie shell. Cut butter into small pieces; dot over apple filling.

4 Preheat oven to 220°C/425°F/gas 7. Roll out remaining dough as before; place over filling. Trim dough edge, leaving 2.5 cm/1 inch overhang. Fold overhang under; make Sharp Fluted or other Decorative Pastry Edge (pages 66-67).

Cheese and apples make good partners; here cheese leaves are placed under pastry leaves to look – and taste – good

5 Reroll dough trimmings. With floured leaf-shaped biscuit cutter or knife, cut 7 leaves, rerolling dough if necessary. Arrange leaves on top of pie. Lightly brush top of pie with milk.

6 With tip of knife, cut hole in top crust to allow steam to escape during baking.

7 Evenly sprinkle caster sugar over pie. Set pie dish on baking sheet and bake for 45 minutes or until pastry is golden and apples are tender.

8 Transfer pie to wire rack; cool slightly. If using cheese slices, cut each slice into leaf shape using biscuit cutter or knife. Gently tuck cheese leaves under pastry leaves, taking care not to break pastry.

CUSTARD PEACH PIE

 8 servings

Allow 3 hours preparation and cooking time

Pastry

Shortcrust Pastry for Pie Shell (see Box, page 64)

Filling

5 medium-sized peaches (about 700 g/1 ½ lb)

150 ml/ ¼ pint soured cream

3 egg yolks

200 g/7 oz caster sugar

30 g/1 oz plain flour

Streusel Topping

60 g/2 oz butter

75 g/2 ½ oz plain flour

60 g/2 oz caster sugar

½ teaspoon ground cinnamon

1 Prepare pastry dough.

2 Preheat oven to 220°C/425°F/gas 7. On lightly floured surface, with floured rolling pin, roll out dough into round about 4 cm/1 ½ inches larger all round than upside-down shallow 20-23 cm/8-9 inch pie dish; ease dough into pie dish to line evenly.

3 Trim dough edge, leaving 2.5 cm/1 inch overhang. Fold overhang under; make Fluted or other Decorative Pastry Edge (pages 66-67).

4 Peel 4 peaches (see Box, page 37); cut peaches into 5 mm/ ¼ inch-thick slices with sharp knife.

5 In pie shell, arrange peach slices in concentric circles, overlapping them slightly.

6 In medium bowl, beat soured cream, egg yolks, sugar and flour just until blended; pour slowly over peaches in pie dish, taking care not to dislodge them.

7 Bake pie for 30 minutes, or just until custard mixture is beginning to set.

8 Meanwhile, prepare streusel topping: in small bowl, rub together butter, flour and sugar until mixture resembles coarse crumbs. Stir in ground cinnamon.

STREUSEL TOPPING

Streusel is a crisp topping of flour, butter and sugar, often mixed with spices such as cinnamon, nutmeg and cloves, which is sprinkled on breads, cakes and puddings before baking. The topping is of German origin, and is very similar to crumble toppings for fruit.

9 After pie has baked for 30 minutes, evenly sprinkle streusel topping over peaches and custard.

Sprinkling streusel topping over peaches and custard

10 Bake for 15 minutes longer or until streusel is golden and knife inserted in centre of pie comes out clean.

11 If pastry browns too quickly, cover edge loosely with foil.

12 Cool pie on wire rack for 1 hour; serve warm, or cool completely to serve cold later.

At end of baking time, insert tip of knife into centre of pie; if custard is set, tip of knife will come out clean

TO SERVE
*Cut remaining peach
into 5 mm/¹/₄ inch thick
slices; use to decorate
centre of pie.*

PARISIENNE APPLE PIES

6 servings
Allow 2 hours
preparation and
cooking time

Pastry

375 g/13 oz plain flour

225 g/8 oz unsalted butter,
softened

75 g/2 1/2 oz caster sugar

2 egg yolks, lightly beaten

1 tablespoon milk

Filling

8 large Golden Delicious
apples

100 g/3 1/2 oz caster sugar
plus extra for sprinkling

60 g/2 oz unsalted butter

1 Prepare pastry dough: in large bowl, with fingertips, quickly mix flour, butter and sugar until mixture resembles coarse crumbs. Add egg yolks and milk; mix until dough will hold together.

2 Shape two-thirds of dough into ball; wrap and set aside. On non-stick baking parchment, with rolling pin, roll out remaining one-third of dough 3 mm/1/8 inch thick. With 6 x 4 cm/ 2 1/2 x 1 1/2 inch leaf-shaped biscuit cutter, cut out 36 leaves. With cocktail stick, press 'vein' into each leaf; place on baking sheet and refrigerate.

3 Divide larger ball of dough into 6 equal pieces. Press one piece of dough on to bottom and up side of each of six 10-11 cm/4-4 1/2 inch loose-bottomed tartlet tins; refrigerate.

4 Prepare filling: peel and core apples; cut into 5 mm/1/4 inch thick slices. In large frying pan over medium-high heat, heat sugar and butter until butter melts, stirring occasionally (do not use margarine because it separates from sugar during cooking). Sugar will not be completely dissolved.

5 Arrange apple slices on top of sugar mixture; heat to boiling (do not stir). Cook for about 20 minutes, depending on juiciness of apples, until sugar mixture is caramel-coloured; stir to mix apples with caramelized sugar. (Apples should still be slightly crunchy.) Remove pan from heat.

6 Preheat oven to 200°C/400°F/gas 6. Spoon apple mixture into tartlet shells. Arrange 6 dough leaves on top of each pie, leaving some of filling uncovered. Arrange apple pies in baking tray for easier handling. Bake pies for 25-30 minutes until pastry is golden (cover leaves with foil after 15 minutes, if necessary, to prevent overbrowning).

7 Cool pies on wire rack for 10 minutes; lightly sprinkle with caster sugar. Serve warm, or cool completely to serve cold later. Remove sides and bases of tins before serving.

Parisienne Apple Pies are lightly dusted with caster sugar just before serving, to give pastry leaves a frosted look

Pies are baked in fluted, loose-bottomed tartlet tins so they can be removed from tins before serving; this way they look their best for serving

TARTS AND FLANS

Tarts and flans – crisp, rich and sweet pastry filled with creamy custards, juicy fresh fruits, fine chocolate and crunchy nuts – make the most delectable of desserts. In this collection of recipes you will find old favourites as well as new and exciting ideas, each one of them as good to look at as it is to eat, and you don't have to be a pastry chef to make them!

TART OR FLAN SHELL

| 175 g/6 oz plain flour |
| 1 tablespoon caster sugar |
| ¼ teaspoon salt (optional) |
| 120 g/4 oz cold butter |
| 2-3 tablespoons cold water |

1 In medium bowl, with fork, stir flour with sugar and salt, if using. With pastry blender or with fingertips, cut or rub butter into flour mixture until mixture resembles coarse crumbs.

2 Sprinkle cold water, a tablespoon at a time, into mixture, mixing lightly with fork after each addition, until dough just holds together. With hands, shape dough into ball. Wrap and refrigerate for 1 hour.

3 Preheat oven to 220°C/425°F/gas 7. On lightly floured surface, with floured rolling pin, roll out dough into round about 2.5 cm/1 inch larger all round than 23-25 cm/ 9-10 inch loose-bottomed tart or flan tin.

4 Ease dough into tin to line evenly; press dough on to bottom and up side of tin.

5 Roll rolling pin across top of tin to trim off excess dough; reserve trimmings for decoration.

6 With fork, prick dough liberally to prevent puffing and shrinkage during baking.

7 Line shell with foil; fill with dried or baking beans. Bake shell for 10 minutes. Remove foil and beans; again prick dough. Bake shell for 10-15 minutes longer until golden brown.

8 If pastry puffs up, gently press it to tin with spoon.

9 Cool tart or flan shell in tin on wire rack.

TARTLET SHELLS

1 In bowl, with fork, stir 75 g/2 ½ oz plain flour, 1 teaspoon caster sugar and ¼ teaspoon salt (optional). With pastry blender or fingertips, cut or rub 60 g/2 oz cold butter into flour mixture until mixture resembles coarse crumbs. Sprinkle 4-5 teaspoons cold water, a teaspoon at a time, into mixture, mixing lightly with fork after each addition until dough is just moist enough to hold together. With hands, shape dough into ball. Wrap and refrigerate for 1 hour.

2 Preheat oven to 190°C/375°F/gas 5. On lightly floured surface, with floured rolling pin, roll out half of the dough 3 mm/ ⅛ inch thick. With floured 7.5 cm/3 inch round pastry cutter, cut out as many rounds as possible. Repeat with remaining dough and trimmings to make 18 rounds.

3 Press each round of dough on to bottom and up side of eighteen 6 cm/2 ½ inch round tartlet tins (2 cm/ ¾ inch deep).

4 With fork, prick tartlet shells in many places to prevent puffing and shrinkage during baking. Place tartlet tins in baking tray for easy handling. Bake for 12-15 minutes until lightly browned.

5 Cool tartlet shells in tins on wire racks for 10 minutes. With knife, gently loosen tartlet shells from sides of tins; remove from tins and cool completely on wire racks.

6 If not using tartlet shells immediately, store them in airtight container.

FRENCH APPLE PUFFS

🍴 8 servings
🕐 Allow 1 ½ hours preparation and cooking time

450 g/1 lb frozen puff pastry

4 medium-sized dessert apples

3 digestive biscuits, finely crushed

45 g/1 ½ oz butter, melted

About 3 tablespoons orange marmalade

Icing sugar for sprinkling

Whipped cream for serving (optional)

1 Thaw puff pastry according to packet instructions.

2 Preheat oven to 220°C/425°F/gas 7. On floured surface, with floured rolling pin, roll half of the pastry out to 36 cm/14 ½ inch square.

3 Using 17.5 cm/7 inch round plate as a guide, cut out 4 rounds from pastry square.

4 Cut 2 apples in half lengthways; remove cores and peel. Cut apple halves lengthways into paper-thin slices.

5 Place pastry rounds on large baking sheet. Top each pastry round with 1 tablespoon biscuit crumbs, then with one-quarter of the apple slices.

Finely crushed digestive biscuits add crunch to apple filling, and help prevent apple juices seeping into pastry and making it soggy

---

TO SERVE
Sift icing sugar over apple slices. Serve puffs warm, with whipped cream.

---

6 Brush apple slices with some melted butter.

7 Bake apple puffs for 15 minutes or until pastry is lightly browned and crisp and apple slices are tender. With fish slice, transfer apple puffs to wire racks.

8 In small saucepan over low heat, heat orange marmalade until melted. Brush over apple slices while they are still hot.

9 Repeat with remaining ingredients to make 4 more apple puffs.

Icing sugar melts and caramelizes on hot marmalade glaze

PLUM AND ALMOND FLAN

8 servings
Allow 3 hours
preparation and
cooking time

Cinnamon Shortbread

175 g/6 oz plain flour
120 g/4 oz butter, softened
60 g/2 oz caster sugar
1/2 teaspoon ground cinnamon

Filling

700 g/1 1/2 lb Victoria plums
100 g/3 1/2 oz caster sugar
1 tablespoon cornflour
1/2 teaspoon ground cinnamon
1/4 teaspoon almond essence
30 g/1 oz slivered blanched almonds
Whipped cream for serving (optional)

Flan case is rich and buttery, more like shortbread than pastry

1 Prepare cinnamon shortbread dough: in medium bowl, combine flour, butter, sugar and cinnamon. With fingertips, mix until dough just holds together.

2 Press shortbread on to bottom and up side of 20 cm/8 inch loose-bottomed tart or flan tin.

3 Preheat oven to 190°C/375°F/gas 5. Prepare filling: cut each plum in half and remove stone; slice plums.

4 In large bowl, toss plums, sugar, corn-flour, cinnamon and almond essence.

5 Arrange plum slices, closely overlapping, to form concentric circles in shortbread shell.

PLUMS

These plump, fragrant fruits are in season from the beginning of May until the end of October, but are at their plentiful best in August.

- Plums come in a wide range of sizes, shapes and colours, with skin ranging from bright yellow-green to reddish-purple to purplish-black, depending on variety.

- It doesn't matter which variety of plum you choose for cooking – all types of plum can be used interchangeably in recipes, including damsons and greengages.

- A perfect plum is richly coloured and firm, with a slight softening at stalk end.

- Five or six plums weigh 450 g/1 lb.

- Store ripe plums in refrigerator, for 3-5 days.

- Plums can be frozen – halve and remove stones, then freeze plums in small quantities in freezer bags.

Sprinkling almonds over plums

6 Evenly sprinkle slivered almonds over plum slices.

7 Bake in the oven for 45 minutes or until pastry is golden and plums are tender. Cool flan in tin on wire rack.

8 Carefully remove side of tin. Transfer flan to serving plate.

9 Serve Plum and Almond Flan cut into wedges, with whipped cream if you like.

ASCOT FRUIT TART

🥄 8 servings
⏱ Allow 3 ½ hours preparation and cooking time

Coconut Pastry

150 g/5 oz plain flour

75 g/2 ½ oz shredded or desiccated coconut

90 g/3 oz butter

30 g/1 oz caster sugar

1 egg yolk

Lemon Custard Filling

1 large lemon

90 g/3 oz butter

60 g/2 oz caster sugar

1 tablespoon cornflour

4 egg yolks

300 ml/ ½ pint double or whipping cream

Fruit Topping

350 g/12 oz raspberries

225 g/8 oz blueberries

1 Prepare coconut pastry dough: in medium bowl, combine flour, coconut, butter, sugar and egg yolk. With fingertips, mix together just until blended.

2 Press dough on to bottom and up side of 25 cm/10 inch loose-bottomed tart or flan tin. With fork, prick pastry shell in many places to prevent puffing and shrinkage during baking.

3 Preheat oven to 180°C/350°F/gas 4. Line pastry shell with foil and spread evenly with dried or baking beans; bake for 10 minutes. Remove beans and foil; again prick dough. Bake for 10-15 minutes longer until golden (if pastry puffs up, press it to tin with spoon). Cool pastry shell in tin on wire rack.

4 While pastry shell is baking, prepare lemon custard filling: from lemon, grate 1 teaspoon zest and squeeze 2 tablespoons juice; set aside. In heavy medium saucepan over medium-low heat, heat butter, sugar and cornflour, stirring constantly, until mixture thickens and boils; boil for 1 minute longer.

5 In small bowl, with fork, beat egg yolks; stir in small amount of hot sugar mixture.

6 Slowly pour egg yolk mixture back into sugar mixture in pan, stirring rapidly with wooden spoon to prevent lumping.

7 Cook, stirring constantly, until mixture thickens and coats spoon well, about 1 minute. Remove saucepan from heat.

8 Stir lemon zest and lemon juice into custard; cool, then cover and refrigerate until very cold, about 1 hour.

9 In small bowl, whip double or whipping cream until stiff peaks form. With rubber spatula or wire whisk, fold whipped cream into chilled lemon custard.

RASPBERRIES

These small, juicy, thimble-shaped berries come in red and yellow varieties, and are best during June to July and September to October.

• Choose plump, fresh-looking berries.

• Do not buy berries that are crushed or bruised, or that have leaked moisture through container.

• Keep refrigerated and use within 1-2 days.

• Eat raspberries plain or use in fruit salads, pies, flans, crumbles, jams, jellies and sweet sauces.

10 Evenly spoon lemon custard filling into cooled pastry shell.

Spooning lemon custard filling into pastry shell

Whipped cream is folded into egg custard to make this rich filling

11 Arrange raspberries in circular pattern round edge of tart.

12 Fill in centre with blueberries and raspberries; refrigerate for 1 hour until custard is set.

With different fruits to match the seasons, this can be a year-round treat. Use bananas and oranges in winter; pineapple and papaya in spring; apricots and cherries in summer; grapes and pears in autumn. Slice or dice fruit as necessary, to make it look as pretty as possible, and for easy serving

FRUIT TARTLETS

Petite and prettily shaped, tartlets filled with a variety of colourful fruits and topped with a sparkling glaze make an irresistible display on the table. Here are a few ideas for presentation, to inspire you to create your own filling and topping combinations. Use tartlet tins of as many different shapes as you can, and choose small whole fruits that lend themselves to the shape of the shells, or cut up larger fruits to fit. Make the pastry shells from the recipe for Tartlet Shells (see Box, page 77), leave them to cool, then fill them with Lemon Custard Filling (page 80) or sweetened whipped cream. Once fruits have been arranged on top, brush them with a little melted jelly – use redcurrant jelly for dark fruits, or sieved apricot jam for light-coloured fruits. The thin glaze will provide an instant gloss and keep fruit looking its best for a few hours if necessary.

Raspberry and blackberry

Blueberry

Strawberry

Orange and grapefruit

Red and green seedless grapes

FRUIT TOPPINGS

Choose fruits that suit the size and shape of the tartlet shell. Dainty small whole fruits such as berries and grapes can be used singly, or heaped or clustered on filling. Dice larger fruits, or cut them into slices for dramatic effect.

Grapes can be left whole or sliced, according to their size

Star fruit slices have a beautiful shape

Passion fruit pulp can be sprinkled over other fruits as a decoration

PEAR CRUMBLE TART

8-10 servings
Allow 3 hours preparation and cooking time

Filling

30 g/1 oz caster sugar
1 teaspoon ground cinnamon
300 ml/ ½ pint double or whipping cream
2 egg yolks
2 x 400 g/14 oz cans pear halves

Crumble Crust

215 g/7 ½ oz plain flour
¼ teaspoon salt (optional)
45 g/1 ½ oz caster sugar
90 g/3 oz butter

Crumble base is rich, sweet and buttery, with a short texture

Pear slices are set in a creamy egg custard, subtly flavoured with cinnamon

1 Prepare filling: in small bowl, with fork, mix sugar and cinnamon; set aside.

2 In another small bowl, with wire whisk or fork, beat double or whipping cream with egg yolks until blended; cover and refrigerate.

3 Preheat oven to 200°C/400°F/gas 6. Prepare crumble crust: in medium bowl, with fork, stir flour, salt, if using, and sugar. With pastry blender or with fingertips, cut or rub butter into flour mixture until mixture resembles coarse crumbs. (Mixture will be dry and crumbly.)

4 With hand, firmly press crumble mixture on to bottom and up side of shallow 25 cm/10 inch pie dish.

5 Drain pears; pat dry with kitchen paper. Slice pears, then arrange in pie dish, fanning slices slightly.

6 Over pear slices in bottom of crumble crust, with spoon, evenly sprinkle sugar and cinnamon mixture.

7 Bake tart for about 5 minutes or until sugar and cinnamon mixture is melted.

8 With pie dish still on oven rack, carefully pour cream mixture over pears.

9 Bake tart for 20-30 minutes until top is browned and knife inserted in centre of filling comes out clean.

10 Cool tart in dish on wire rack. Serve warm, or cover and refrigerate to serve cold later.

UPSIDE-DOWN APPLE TART

8-10 servings
Allow 1 ½ hours preparation and cooking time

300 g/10 oz frozen puff pastry

10 large Golden Delicious apples

200 g/7 oz caster sugar

120 g/4 oz butter

¼ teaspoon almond essence

Chilled pouring cream for serving (optional)

1 Thaw puff pastry according to packet instructions.

2 Meanwhile, peel and core apples (Golden Delicious apples with very green skin retain their shape best; do not use other apples). Cut each apple in half lengthways.

3 In 25 cm/ 10 inch heavy frying pan with metal handle (or with handle covered with heavy-duty foil) over medium heat, heat sugar, butter and almond essence until butter melts, stirring occasionally (do not use margarine because it will separate from sugar during cooking). Sugar will not be completely dissolved. Remove pan from heat.

4 Arrange apple halves on their sides round side and in centre of pan, fitting apples very tightly together.

5 Return frying pan to medium heat and bring to the boil; boil for 20-40 minutes, depending on juiciness of apples, until butter and sugar mixture becomes caramel-coloured. Remove from heat.

6 Preheat oven to 230°C/450°F/gas 8.

7 On lightly floured surface, with floured rolling pin, roll pastry out to 30 cm/12 inch round.

8 Carefully place pastry round over apple halves in frying pan.

9 With prongs of fork, press pastry to edge of frying pan.

10 Cut slits in pastry. Bake in the oven for 20-25 minutes until pastry is golden. Remove pan from oven; allow to cool on wire rack for 10 minutes.

11 Place dessert platter upside-down over frying pan; holding them firmly together, carefully invert tart on to dessert platter (do this over sink since tart may be extremely juicy).

> **TO SERVE**
> Serve Upside-Down Apple Tart warm or cold, with chilled cream if you like.

When tart is turned out upside-down for serving, apples are caramelized yet still retain their shape

FRESH CHERRY FLAN

🍴 8 servings
⏲ Allow 2 hours preparation and cooking time

1 x 25 cm/10 inch Tart or Flan Shell (see Box, page 77)

450 g/1 lb cherries

3 eggs

300 ml/ ½ pint double or whipping cream

60 g/2 oz caster sugar

2 tablespoons almond liqueur or 1 teaspoon almond essence

For the best creamy texture, egg custard should be firm and set at edge when removed from oven, but still slightly soft in centre; it will set throughout if left to stand for 10-15 minutes

1 Prepare and bake Tart or Flan Shell according to recipe instructions; cool. Turn oven down to 180°C/350°F/gas 4.

2 Meanwhile, with cherry stoner, remove stones from cherries.

3 In large bowl, with electric mixer, beat eggs with double or whipping cream, sugar and almond liqueur or almond essence until blended.

CUSTARDS AND CUSTARD TARTS

Because custards are so delicate in texture, and can easily be overcooked, they should be removed from the oven when they are set at the sides – and still slightly soft in the centre.

Testing Custards
When custard looks firm and set, double-check by inserting knife 2.5 cm/1 inch from edge – custard is ready if knife comes out clean. Custard will continue cooking after it has been removed from the oven, so that after 10-15 minutes it will be set throughout.

4 Place cherries in pastry shell, arranging them in concentric circles.

5 Set tin on oven rack and slowly pour egg mixture over cherries, taking care not to dislodge pattern.

6 Bake flan in the oven for 30 minutes or until knife inserted in filling 2.5 cm/ 1 inch from edge comes out clean.

7 Cool flan slightly in tin on wire rack.

8 Remove side of tin. Serve flan warm, or cover and leave to cool to serve cold later.

Sweet juicy cherries are stoned and set in an almond-flavoured creamy egg custard

CLAFOUTIS FLAN

🍴 8-10 servings
⏱ Allow 4 hours preparation and cooking time

Pastry

215 g/7 ¹/₂ oz plain flour

³/₄ teaspoon salt (optional)

1 teaspoon caster sugar

120 g/4 oz butter, softened

1 egg

Filling

6 eggs

200 g/7 oz caster sugar

450 ml/ ³/₄ pint milk

150 ml/ ¹/₄ pint soured cream

1 teaspoon vanilla essence

175 g/6 oz blueberries or stoned cherries

1 Prepare pastry dough: in medium bowl, with fork, stir flour, salt, if using, and sugar. With pastry blender or with fingertips, cut or rub butter into flour mixture until mixture resembles coarse crumbs. In cup, with fork, beat egg; add to flour mixture and mix lightly with fork until dough just holds together, adding a little water if necessary. With hands, shape dough into ball. Wrap and refrigerate for 1 hour.

Here, fresh blueberries are used for this French 'clafoutis', but you can use stoned cherries if they are more easy to obtain

2 On lightly floured surface, with floured rolling pin, roll out dough into round 2.5 cm/1 inch larger all round than 30 cm/12 inch flan dish. Ease dough into dish to line evenly; trim edge. With fork, prick pastry shell in many places to prevent puffing during baking. To prevent pastry from shrinking during baking, place shell in freezer for 15 minutes.

3 Preheat oven to 220°C/425°F/gas 7. Line pastry shell with foil and evenly spread dried or baking beans over bottom.

4 Bake pastry shell for 20 minutes. Remove beans and foil and again prick pastry shell. Bake for a further 3-4 minutes until pastry is lightly browned and no longer soft and raw (if pastry puffs up, gently press it to dish with spoon).

5 Prepare filling: in large bowl, with electric mixer, beat eggs and caster sugar until very thick and lemon-coloured, about 3 minutes. Gradually add milk, soured cream and vanilla essence; beat until well blended.

6 Place blueberries or cherries in warm pastry shell. Slowly pour over egg mixture.

7 Bake in the oven for 30-35 minutes until filling is set and pastry is golden brown; cover with foil after 20 minutes to prevent overbrowning.

8 Cool flan in dish on wire rack.

Pouring egg mixture over blueberries

Flan is served topped with extra blueberries and sifted with icing sugar

DELUXE APPLE FLAN

This beautiful apple flan is a classic piece of French pâtisserie, yet it is easy to make at home. Take care to cut the apple slices really thinly, and take time to arrange them in overlapping circles; your efforts will be rewarded.

8-10 servings
Allow 4 hours preparation and cooking time

Pastry

150 g/5 oz plain flour	
75 g/2 ¹/₂ oz butter, softened	
30 g/1 oz caster sugar	
¹/₈ teaspoon salt (optional)	

Filling

6 large dessert apples	
120 g/4 oz apricot jam	
1 teaspoon lemon juice	

1 Prepare pastry dough: in medium bowl, combine flour, butter, sugar, salt, if using, and *2 tablespoons cold water*. With fingertips, mix together just until blended, adding more water, 1 teaspoon at a time, if needed.

2 Press dough on to bottom and up side of 23 cm/9 inch loose-bottomed tart or flan tin; refrigerate.

3 Prepare filling: peel and core 3 apples; cut into chunks. In saucepan, cook apple chunks with half of the apricot jam and *4 tablespoons water* until apples are tender.

4 In food processor or blender, blend apple mixture until smooth. Pour apple purée into medium non-stick saucepan; cook, uncovered, until very thick, stirring frequently to prevent purée catching on bottom of pan.

5 Peel remaining 3 apples. Cut each apple into quarters lengthways; remove cores.

Removing cores from apples

FILLING AND GLAZING FLAN

Spreading apple purée in pastry shell: *spoon apple purée into pastry shell, then spread evenly with back of spoon.*

Arranging apples in centre of flan: *place apple slices, closely overlapping, in small circle in centre of apple purée filling.*

Arranging remaining apple slices: *place remaining apple slices, closely overlapping, in large circle round first small circle, to cover apple purée completely and fill pastry shell.*

Glazing apples: *with pastry brush, gently spread hot apricot glaze over apple slices until evenly coated.*

6 Cut each quarter lengthways into 3 mm/⅛ inch thick slices.

7 In large bowl, gently toss apple slices with lemon juice.

8 Preheat oven to 200°C/400°F/gas 6.

9 Fill pastry shell with apple purée and cover with apple slices (see Box, page 88).

10 Bake flan in the oven for 45 minutes or until apple slices are tender and browned. Transfer tin to wire rack.

11 In small saucepan, melt remaining apricot jam; with spoon, press through sieve if liked.

12 Brush jam glaze evenly over apple slices (see Box, page 88). Cool flan in tin on wire rack.

13 To serve, carefully remove side of tin.

LEMON CUSTARD TART

🍴 8 servings
⏰ Make day before and keep in refrigerator

Pastry

90 g/3 oz butter, softened

45 g/1 ¹/2 oz caster sugar

¹/2 teaspoon grated lemon zest

1 egg yolk

120 g/4 oz plain flour

Filling

4 eggs

4 egg yolks

175 ml/6 fl oz lemon juice

190 g/6 ¹/2 oz caster sugar

60 g/2 oz butter

2 tablespoons apricot jam

Lemon slices to decorate

1 Prepare pastry dough: in medium bowl, with electric mixer, beat butter, sugar and lemon zest until well blended; beat in egg yolk. Stir in flour until just blended. Shape pastry dough into ball; wrap and refrigerate for 1 hour.

2 Preheat oven to 220°C/425°F/gas 7. On lightly floured surface, with floured rolling pin, roll out dough into round 2.5 cm/1 inch larger all round than 23 cm/9 inch loose-bottomed tart or flan tin. Ease dough into tin to line evenly; trim edge even with rim. With fork, prick pastry shell in many places to prevent puffing and shrinkage during baking. Line pastry shell with foil and spread evenly with dried or baking beans.

3 Bake pastry shell for 10 minutes; remove beans and foil and again prick shell. Bake for a further 5 minutes or until pastry is golden (if pastry puffs up, gently press it to tin with spoon). Cool pastry shell in tin on wire rack.

4 Prepare filling: in non-stick saucepan, with wire whisk or fork, beat eggs and egg yolks until blended; stir in lemon juice and 150 g/5 oz sugar. Cook over medium-low heat, stirring constantly, until mixture thickens and coats a spoon well, about 15 minutes (do not boil or mixture will curdle). Stir in butter until melted.

5 Into baked pastry shell, pour lemon custard filling.

6 Refrigerate tart overnight so that filling is well chilled and firm.

Here lemon is 'vandyked' with canelle knife before slicing to make cartwheel shapes

7 About 1-2 hours before serving, preheat grill to high. Cover edge of pastry shell with foil to prevent overbrowning. Evenly sprinkle remaining caster sugar over chilled lemon custard filling.

8 Place tart under grill for 6-8 minutes until sugar melts and begins to brown, making a shiny crust. (Take care not to let filling scorch.) Cool, then refrigerate.

9 Carefully remove side of tin; slide tart on to cake plate. Melt apricot jam, then work through sieve. Brush top of tart with jam glaze and decorate with lemon slices.

PASTRIES

All pastries are made with some kind of dough; and the different doughs, coupled with the wide variety of fillings that can be used, add up to an almost limitless choice of eye-catching, taste-tempting desserts. Melt-in-the-mouth shortcrust can be used for fruit-filled rolls and dumplings.

Flaky puff pastry makes handsome pies, tarts and turnovers. Light and airy shells made from choux pastry take to luscious fillings from whipped cream to ice cream; and delicious desserts made with paper-thin phyllo range from classic Strudel to the incomparable Baklava.

PEARS EN CROÛTE À LA CRÈME

Makes 6
Allow 1 ½ hours preparation and cooking time

Filling

15 g/ ½ oz caster sugar

¼ teaspoon ground cinnamon

3 medium-sized William's pears

6 whole cloves

Pastry

215 g/7 ½ oz plain flour

120 g/4 oz butter, softened

1 x 85 g/3 oz package full-fat soft cheese, softened

1 egg white

Custard

1 egg yolk

450 ml/ ¾ pint single or half cream

4 teaspoons cornflour

45 g/1 ½ oz caster sugar

¼ teaspoon almond essence

1 Prepare filling: in cup, with fork, stir sugar with cinnamon; set aside. Peel pears. Cut each pear in half lengthways; remove cores.

2 Prepare pastry dough: in medium bowl, combine flour, butter and soft cheese; with fingertips, mix together just until blended.

3 On lightly floured surface, with floured rolling pin, roll out half of the dough 3 mm/⅛ inch thick. Using 18 cm/7 inch round plate as a guide, cut 3 rounds from dough; reserve trimmings.

4 Sprinkle rounds of dough with half of the sugar and cinnamon mixture; place a pear half, cut side up, on each round. Carefully fold round of dough over each pear half. Pinch dough edges to seal.

5 Place wrapped pears, seam side down, on ungreased large baking sheet. Repeat with remaining pears and dough to make 6 altogether.

Pastry made with soft cheese is rich and melt-in-the mouth, an ideal casing for a sweet William's pear

6 Preheat oven to 190°C/375°F/gas 5. Reroll dough trimmings; cut to make leaves. Brush dough with egg white; decorate with dough leaves and brush them with egg white.

7 Bake pears for 35 minutes or until pastry is golden. Transfer to wire rack; cool slightly.

8 Meanwhile, make custard: in medium saucepan, combine egg yolk, single or half cream, cornflour and sugar.

9 Cook over medium-low heat, stirring constantly, until mixture thickens and coats a spoon well, about 15 minutes. Remove saucepan from heat; stir in almond essence. Cool custard slightly.

> *TO SERVE*
> *On to each of 6 dessert plates, spoon some custard. Place pear in centre of custard; insert whole clove in tip of each to resemble stalk. Or refrigerate pears and custard separately to serve chilled later.*

BAKLAVA

Makes 24
Allow 3 ½ hours preparation and cooking time

450 g/1 lb walnut pieces, finely chopped

100 g/3 ½ oz caster sugar

1 teaspoon ground cinnamon

450 g/1 lb fresh or frozen (thawed) phyllo pastry

225 g/8 oz butter, melted

350 g/12 oz liquid honey

In Baklava, layer upon layer of phyllo pastry and chopped walnuts are made sweet and sticky with melted butter and honey

1 In large bowl, with fork, mix finely chopped walnuts, sugar and cinnamon; set aside.

2 Cut sheets of phyllo into 33 x 23 cm/ 13 x 9 inch rectangles. In greased 33 x 23 cm/ 13 x 9 inch baking dish, place 1 phyllo sheet; brush with some melted butter. Repeat with more phyllo and butter until there are 6 rectangular sheets of phyllo in dish.

3 Over phyllo pastry in baking dish, sprinkle one-quarter of chopped walnut mixture.

4 Repeat steps 2 and 3 to make 3 more layers (4 layers in total). Place remaining phyllo on top of last amount of walnuts; brush with butter.

5 Preheat oven to 150°C/300°F/gas 2. With sharp knife, cut just halfway through layers in triangle pattern to make 24 servings (cut lengthways into 3 strips; cut each strip crossways into 4 rectangles; then cut each rectangle diagonally into 2 triangles).

6 Bake for 1 hour and 25 minutes or until top is golden brown.

7 In small saucepan over medium-low heat, heat honey until hot but not boiling. Evenly spoon hot honey over hot Baklava.

ALTERNATIVE SHAPES

For a change from triangles, you can cut Baklava into diamond shapes, which are more traditional.

Diamond Baklava
In step 5, with sharp knife, cut just halfway through layers in diamond pattern (cut lengthways into 4 strips, then cut diagonally across strips in parallel lines); finish cutting through layers in step 9.

Spooning honey over Baklava

8 Cool Baklava in dish on wire rack for at least 1 hour; cover with foil and leave at room temperature until serving.

9 To serve, with sharp knife, finish cutting through layers to make 24 Baklava triangles.

APPLE STRUDEL

🥄 10 servings
⏱ Allow 2 hours preparation and cooking time

3 large cooking apples

100 g/3 ¹/₂ oz caster sugar

75 g/2 ¹/₂ oz seedless raisins

60 g/2 oz walnut pieces, chopped

¹/₂ teaspoon ground cinnamon

¹/₄ teaspoon grated nutmeg

About 75 g/2 ¹/₂ oz white breadcrumbs

225 g/8 oz fresh or frozen (thawed) phyllo pastry

120 g/4 oz butter, melted

Icing sugar for sprinkling

Icing sugar is sifted over top of strudel to help hide cracks in phyllo pastry

1 Grease large baking sheet. Peel, core and thinly slice apples. In bowl, toss apples with caster sugar, raisins, walnuts, cinnamon, nutmeg and 25 g/³/₄ oz breadcrumbs.

2 Cut two 60 cm/24 inch lengths of greaseproof paper. Place 2 long sides together, overlapping them by about 5 cm/2 inches; join with adhesive tape.

3 On sheet of grease-proof paper, arrange 1 sheet of phyllo. (It should be a 43 x 30 cm/ 17 x 10 inch rectangle; if necessary, trim or overlap small pieces of phyllo to make it this size.) Brush with some melted butter.

4 Sprinkle phyllo with scant tablespoon breadcrumbs. Continue layering phyllo, brushing each sheet with melted butter and sprinkling every other sheet with crumbs.

Spooning apple mixture on to phyllo

5 Preheat oven to 190°C/375°F/gas 5. Spoon apple mixture along 1 long side of phyllo rectangle to within 1 cm/ ¹/₂ inch of edges to cover about half of rectangle.

6 From apple mixture side, roll phyllo, Swiss roll fashion, using grease-proof to help lift roll.

7 Place roll on baking sheet, seam side down. Brush with remaining melted butter. Bake for 40 minutes or until golden. Cool on baking sheet for 30 minutes.

CONTINENTAL FRUIT SLICE

🍴 8 servings
⏱ Allow 4 hours preparation and cooking time

Filling

225 g/8 oz dried figs, coarsely chopped

150 g/5 oz stoned dates, coarsely chopped

120 g/4 oz dried apricots, coarsely chopped

30 g/1 oz sultanas

2 tablespoons lemon juice

1 teaspoon ground cinnamon

100 g/3 ½ oz caster sugar

120 g/4 oz walnut pieces, chopped

Pastry

300 g/10 oz plain flour

1 teaspoon salt (optional)

30 g/1 oz caster sugar

175 g/6 oz butter

1 egg

1 tablespoon milk

1 Make filling: in large saucepan over high heat, bring figs, dates, apricots, sultanas, lemon juice, cinnamon, sugar and *600 ml/1 pint water* to the boil. Reduce heat to low; simmer, uncovered, stirring occasionally, for 30 minutes or until mixture is thick. Remove saucepan from heat; stir in chopped walnuts. Leave to cool for at least 1 hour.

2 Meanwhile, prepare pastry dough: in medium bowl, with fork, stir flour, salt, if using, and sugar. With pastry blender or with fingertips, cut or rub butter into flour mixture until mixture resembles coarse crumbs. Sprinkle *5-6 tablespoons cold water*, a tablespoon at a time, into flour mixture, mixing lightly with fork after each addition until dough just holds together. With hands, shape dough into ball. Wrap and refrigerate until dried fruit filling is cool.

3 Preheat oven to 220°C/425°F/gas 7. Reserve a little dough for making leaves and berries. On lightly floured surface, with floured rolling pin, roll out remaining dough into 40 x 30 cm/ 16 x 12 inch rectangle.

Sweet and juicy filling of dried fruits and nuts is revealed when generous slices are cut for serving

4 Transfer dough rectangle to ungreased large baking sheet. Spoon dried fruit filling lengthways in 10 cm/4 inch wide strip over centre of rectangle to about 6 cm/ 2 ½ inches from each end. Fold one long side of dough rectangle over filling, then roll over to enclose filling, seam side down. Fold dough under on each end of roll.

5 In cup, with fork, beat egg and milk. Brush roll with some egg mixture. With tip of knife, cut few shallow lines in top of roll. On floured surface, with floured rolling pin, roll out reserved dough. With knife, cut out small leaves and roll small pieces of dough into berries. Arrange leaves and berries on top of roll; brush with some egg mixture.

6 Bake roll for 25-30 minutes until pastry is golden. With fish slices, transfer pastry roll to wire rack to cool completely. Serve at room temperature.

PROFITEROLES GLACÉES

Makes 18

Can be made up to 1 month ahead and kept in freezer

Sauce

225 g/8 oz frozen raspberries

60 g/2 oz caster sugar

1 scoop vanilla ice cream

Choux Pastry

60 g/2 oz butter

75 g/2 1/2 oz plain flour

2 eggs

Filling and Topping

60 g/2 oz plain chocolate, broken into pieces

2 tablespoons milk

15 g/ 1/2 oz butter

600 ml/1 pint vanilla ice cream

30 g/1 oz shelled pistachio nuts, chopped

1 Sprinkle raspberries with sugar; set aside to thaw. Preheat oven to 200°C/400°F/gas 6. Grease and flour large baking sheet.

2 Prepare choux pastry dough: in medium saucepan over medium heat, heat butter and 125 ml/4 fl oz water until butter melts and mixture boils. Remove from heat. Add flour all at once; with wooden spoon, vigorously stir until mixture leaves side of pan and forms a ball. Add eggs, 1 at a time, beating well after each addition until dough is smooth and satiny.

3 Drop 18 teaspoonfuls of dough on baking sheet, 5 cm/2 inches apart.

4 Bake for 30 minutes or until golden. Turn oven off; leave puffs in oven for 10 minutes. Cool on wire rack.

5 While puffs are cooling, make sauce: over large bowl, with back of spoon, press and scrape thawed raspberries with their juice firmly against medium-mesh sieve to purée; discard pips left in sieve. Add ice cream to raspberry purée; stir to mix. Cover sauce and refrigerate.

ALTERNATIVE SERVING IDEA

As an alternative to raspberry sauce, you can serve Profiteroles Glacées with other fruit sauces such as strawberry, apricot or mango. This peach sauce goes especially well, both in colour and flavour.

Peach Sauce
In blender at low speed, blend *450 g/1 lb ripe peaches, peeled and stoned, 1/4 teaspoon almond essence* and *1/8 teaspoon grated nutmeg* until all ingredients are smooth.

6 When puffs are cool, make topping: in non-stick saucepan over low heat, heat pieces of chocolate, milk and butter, stirring frequently, until melted and smooth.

7 Cut each puff in half horizontally; fill bottom halves with ice cream; replace tops. Drizzle profiteroles with chocolate mixture and sprinkle with nuts. Freeze.

Profiteroles nestled together on a pool of raspberry sauce are drizzled with chocolate sauce and sprinkled with nuts

TO SERVE
Spoon raspberry sauce on to 6 dessert plates; arrange 3 profiteroles on each plate.

FROZEN DESSERTS

Nothing beats ice cream, frozen yogurt or sorbet for an 'instant' dessert: just dish it up, serve and enjoy. You'll find all your favourite flavours in this chapter, plus recipes to turn them (or their bought counterparts) into chilly treats that money can't buy, such as bombes, frozen cakes and more. For freezer storage, wrap them well to prevent freezer burn, and keep them on hand to serve with easy elegance at very short notice, or to end a feast superbly.

CHESTNUT GLACÉ

🍴 Makes 6

🕐 Allow 15 minutes preparation, plus freezing time

300 ml/ ½ pint double or whipping cream

1 x 439 g/15 ½ oz can unsweetened chestnut purée

120 g/4 oz caster sugar

2 tablespoons brandy

Chocolate Curls (page 58) and lemon leaves (optional) to decorate

1 In small bowl, whip double or whipping cream until stiff peaks form. In large bowl, with fork, mash chestnut purée; stir in sugar and brandy until smooth.

Gold foil tartlet tins give these quick-and-easy frozen desserts a ritzy look

2 With rubber spatula or wire whisk, fold whipped cream into chestnut mixture.

3 Spoon chestnut and cream mixture into foil tartlet tins or small freezerproof ramekins. Cover; freeze until firm, at least 3 hours.

4 Leave to stand at room temperature for about 10 minutes to soften slightly for easier eating.

> *TO SERVE*
> *Decorate with chocolate curls and lemon leaves, if you like.*

FLORIDA FRUIT CUPS

12 servings
Allow 20 minutes preparation, plus freezing time

600 ml/1 pint plain yogurt

3 tablespoons liquid honey

Grated zest of 1 small lemon

300 g/10 oz assorted fresh fruit (halved strawberries, chopped peaches, chopped nectarines, blueberries or raspberries)

Decoration: lemon leaves, halved strawberries, blueberries, raspberries and nectarine wedges

1 Place fluted paper cake cases in each of 12 holes in deep bun tin.

2 Into large bowl, pour yogurt; add honey and grated lemon zest (honey prevents yogurt from crystallizing in freezer). With wire whisk, mix until blended. Gently stir in 175 g/6 oz fruit.

3 Spoon fruit and yogurt mixture into paper cake cases; top with remaining fruit (some fruit will stay above mixture for pretty colour).

4 Cover bun tin; freeze until firm, about 3 hours.

5 With your fingers, carefully peel off paper cake cases from dessert.

Ridges from paper cases look attractive

6 Leave fruit cups to stand at room temperature for 10-15 minutes to soften slightly for easier eating.

> *TO SERVE*
> *Decorate each serving with lemon leaves, strawberry halves, blueberries, raspberries and nectarine wedges.*

VANILLA ICE CREAM

8-10 servings

Allow 30 minutes preparation, plus freezing time

4 eggs, separated

120 g/4 oz vanilla sugar, or caster sugar and 1 teaspoon vanilla essence

300 ml/ 1/2 pint double cream

1 In small bowl, with wire whisk, beat egg yolks until well blended.

2 In large bowl, with electric mixer on full speed, beat egg whites until soft peaks form.

3 Into beaten egg whites, gradually sprinkle vanilla sugar, 1 tablespoon at a time, beating well after each addition. (This will take about 10 minutes.)

4 In another large bowl, whip cream until soft peaks form. (If using vanilla essence, add to cream before whipping.)

5 With rubber spatula or wire whisk, fold beaten egg whites and egg yolks into whipped cream.

6 If you are making one of the variations (see right and Box, right), add the extra ingredients.

7 Turn mixture into 1.5 litre/2 1/2 pint plastic container; cover and freeze overnight.

8 To serve, scoop ice cream into individual dessert bowls or dishes; serve immediately.

SIMPLE VARIATIONS

If you are making one of the following variations on basic vanilla ice cream, use caster sugar instead of vanilla sugar (or omit vanilla essence). Add extra ingredients after folding beaten egg whites and egg yolks into whipped cream.

Ginger Ice Cream
Add *1 teaspoon ground ginger* and *120 g/4 oz stem ginger in syrup, drained and chopped*, to basic ice cream.

Mocha Ice Cream
Add *2 tablespoons coffee essence* and *2 tablespoons coffee liqueur* to basic ice cream.

Fresh Lemon Ice Cream
Add *grated zest* and *juice of 2 lemons* to basic ice cream.

Mango Ice Cream
Peel and stone *1 ripe mango*; lightly mash flesh and add to basic ice cream.

Passion Fruit Ice Cream
Halve *3 passion fruit*; with small spoon, scoop out flesh and add to basic ice cream.

Tutti Frutti Ice Cream
Chop *120 g/4 oz mixed glacé pineapple, raisins, dried apricots, glacé cherries* and *angelica*; in small bowl, soak overnight in *4 tablespoons brandy* to plump them. Add to basic ice cream.

Blackcurrant Ice Cream
Add *3 tablespoons blackcurrant cordial* and *3 tablespoons crème de cassis* to basic ice cream.

SPECIAL VARIATIONS

Once you've mastered the art of ice cream making, you can ring the changes by adding different fresh fruits, chocolate, nuts or fudge to vanilla ice cream. Here are 3 special varieties for you to try.

Chocolate Ice Cream
Make basic vanilla ice cream using caster sugar instead of vanilla sugar (or omit vanilla essence). In small bowl, with spoon, stir *15 g/ 1/2 oz cocoa powder, 30 g/1 oz caster sugar* and about *3 tablespoons boiling water* to a smooth paste; cool. Stir sweetened cocoa paste mixture into ice cream until evenly blended.
Makes 8-10 servings

Fudge-Swirl Ice Cream
Make basic vanilla ice cream using caster sugar instead of vanilla sugar (or omit vanilla essence); freeze until softly set.

Meanwhile, prepare fudge sauce: in heavy saucepan over medium-high heat, bring *200 g/7 oz caster sugar, 300 ml/ 1/2 pint double or whipping cream, 30 g/1 oz butter, 1 tablespoon golden syrup* and *120 g/4 oz plain chocolate, chopped*, to the boil, stirring constantly. Reduce heat to medium; cook for 5 minutes, stirring occasionally. Remove saucepan from heat; stir in *1 teaspoon vanilla essence*.

Leave sauce to cool, stirring occasionally, then with spoon or knife, quickly swirl fudge sauce into ice cream to create marbled design. Cover container of ice cream again, return to freezer and freeze overnight.
Makes 8-10 servings

Strawberry Ice Cream
Make basic vanilla ice cream using caster sugar instead of vanilla sugar (or omit vanilla essence). Add *150 ml/ 1/4 pint strawberry purée*, beating well to mix.
For Raspberry Ice Cream, substitute *raspberry purée* for strawberry. For Gooseberry, Plum or Rhubarb Ice Cream, add *150 ml/ 1/4 pint sweetened cooked gooseberry, plum or rhubarb purée*.
Makes 8-10 servings

Chocolate Ice Cream
A piped chocolate design only hints at the rich taste of Chocolate Ice Cream. Make the designs as shown, using directions for Chocolate Squiggles (page 59); chill and place on servings at the last minute.

Vanilla Ice Cream
Home-made Vanilla Ice Cream is everybody's favourite, so delicious that it can be served absolutely plain. Yet it's equally good topped with sweet sauces, fruit, nuts, honey, liqueur or even crumbled biscuits.

Strawberry Ice Cream
For incomparable flavour, use the reddest, ripest (but not over-ripe), juiciest berries you can find for Strawberry Ice Cream. Here, scoops of varied sizes make a pretty plateful.

Fudge-Swirl Ice Cream
The decoration is built right into Fudge-Swirl Ice Cream, with thick, fudgy sauce rippled through the frozen mixture. Elegant rolled biscuits make a perfect partner.

HAZELNUT ICEBOX CAKE

10 servings
Allow about 2 ½ hours preparation, plus final freezing time

Hazelnut Praline (see Box, below right)

12 egg yolks

175 ml/6 fl oz golden syrup

2 tablespoons coffee liqueur

2 teaspoons instant coffee powder

175 g/6 oz plain chocolate, broken into pieces

750 ml/1 ¼ pints double or whipping cream

Toasted hazelnuts for decoration

1 Prepare Hazelnut Praline.

2 In large bowl, with electric mixer, beat egg yolks and golden syrup until slightly thickened and light-coloured, about 4 minutes.

3 Pour egg yolk mixture into large non-stick saucepan. Cook over low heat, stirring constantly, until mixture thickens and coats a spoon well, about 30 minutes. Remove saucepan from heat.

4 Pour two-thirds of egg yolk mixture into large bowl.

5 In cup, stir coffee liqueur and coffee powder; stir into egg yolk mixture in large bowl.

6 In bowl over pan of gently simmering water, heat half of the chocolate, stirring frequently, until melted and smooth.

7 Stir melted chocolate into remaining egg yolk mixture in saucepan until blended.

8 In another large bowl, whip 600 ml/1 pint double or whipping cream until stiff peaks form.

9 With rubber spatula or wire whisk, fold two-thirds of whipped cream into coffee mixture until blended. Fold remaining whipped cream into chocolate mixture.

10 Spoon half of the coffee mixture into 23 cm/9 inch springform cake tin, spreading evenly; freeze until set, about 15 minutes.

11 Evenly spread chocolate mixture over coffee layer in spring-form tin; freeze until set, about 15 minutes.

12 Sprinkle chocolate layer with hazelnut praline; evenly spread with remaining coffee mixture. Cover and freeze until firm, at least 4 hours.

13 In bowl over pan of gently simmering water, heat remaining chocolate, stirring often, until melted and smooth; remove saucepan from heat. Cut non-stick baking parchment into two 10 cm/4 inch squares. Moisten large baking sheet with water; place parchment squares on baking sheet (water will prevent paper from slipping). Use melted chocolate and parchment squares to make Chocolate Triangles (see Box, page 101); refrigerate.

14 In small bowl, whip remaining double or whipping cream until stiff peaks form. Spoon whipped cream into piping bag fitted with star tube.

HAZELNUT PRALINE

Coarsely chop *135 g/ 4 ½ oz shelled hazelnuts.*

In large frying pan over medium heat, heat *60 g/2 oz caster sugar* until sugar melts and turns golden brown. Stir in chopped hazelnuts; toss to coat well.

Pour into baking tin; leave to cool. Break into small pieces.

15 Run knife or palette knife, dipped in hot water, round edge of springform tin to loosen cake; remove side of tin.

16 Pipe whipped cream into 8 'flowers' round edge on top of cake; place chocolate triangles between whipped cream flowers. Decorate with toasted hazelnuts.

17 Leave cake to stand at room temperature for about 10 minutes for easier slicing.

CHOCOLATE TRIANGLES

Removing baking parchment: *carefully peel parchment from chocolate squares.*

Spreading melted chocolate: *with small palette knife, evenly spread chocolate to cover baking parchment squares. Refrigerate until chocolate is firm but not brittle, about 10 minutes. Remove chocolate from refrigerator; leave to stand for about 5 minutes to soften slightly.*

Cutting triangles: *with sharp knife, quickly but gently cut each chocolate square into 8 triangles.*

Cutting chocolate into triangle shapes

Top of cake is beautifully decorated with whipped cream 'flowers', toasted hazelnuts and chocolate triangles

ICE CREAM BOMBE

8-10 servings
Allow 3 hours preparation, plus final freezing time

3 eggs

90 g/3 oz caster sugar, warmed

75 g/2 ¹/₂ oz self-raising flour

15 g/ ¹/₂ oz cocoa powder

300 ml/ ¹/₂ pint strawberry ice cream

600 ml/1 pint vanilla ice cream

3 tablespoons coffee liqueur (optional)

1 x 425 g/15 oz can stoned black cherries, drained

300 ml/ ¹/₂ pint chocolate ice cream

Chocolate Bow and Ribbon Streamers (see Box, right)

60 g/2 oz desiccated coconut

120 g/4 oz icing sugar, sifted

120 g/4 oz butter, softened

¹/₄ teaspoon vanilla essence

1 Preheat oven to 220°C/425°F/gas 7. Lightly grease 33 x 23 cm/ 13 x 9 inch Swiss roll tin and line with non-stick baking parchment.

2 In large bowl, with electric mixer, beat eggs and caster sugar until very thick and lemon-coloured. Sift over flour and cocoa powder; with large metal spoon, fold into egg mixture. Spoon mixture into tin, spreading evenly. Bake for 10 minutes or until top of cake springs back when lightly touched with finger. Immediately turn cake out on to wire rack; peel off baking parchment and leave cake to cool.

3 Place both strawberry and vanilla ice creams in refrigerator to soften slightly.

4 Line medium bowl with cling film. Cut chocolate cake into pieces to line bowl, keeping large piece aside for top; trim pieces of cake to fit, if necessary and press trimmings into gaps. Brush cake with coffee liqueur.

5 Spoon half of the strawberry ice cream into cake-lined bowl. Spoon one-quarter of vanilla ice cream in dollops on to strawberry ice cream. Scatter one-quarter of cherries between vanilla ice cream dollops.

6 Repeat with remaining strawberry ice cream, one-quarter of vanilla ice cream and one-quarter of cherries; press down mixture to eliminate air pockets. Place bowl in freezer to harden ice cream slightly, about 20 minutes.

DECORATION FOR ICE CREAM BOMBE

The bow and ribbon streamers on the Ice Cream Bombe (page 103) add a professional touch to the finished dessert, yet they are simple to make. If you use white marzipan or almond paste rather than yellow, you will get a better 'chocolate' colour.

Chocolate Bow and Ribbon Streamers

Knead *2 teaspoons sifted cocoa powder* into *120 g/ 4 oz marzipan* or *almond paste* until evenly blended. If mixture seems very dry, lightly dampen hands, but do not use too much water or paste will be too sticky to roll.

Sift *a very little extra cocoa powder* on to work surface; with rolling pin, roll out paste to 20 x 11 cm/ 8 x 4 ¹/₂ inch rectangle.

Trim edges; cut paste into 8 long strips of equal width. Use 5 strips for ribbon streamers; cut ends on the diagonal. Arrange on bombe, some full length and some shorter. Make loops with remaining strips; place on top of bombe to resemble bow.

7 Meanwhile, place chocolate ice cream in refrigerator to soften slightly, and return remaining vanilla ice cream to freezer.

8 Remove bowl from freezer. Repeat layering as for strawberry ice cream, but use chocolate ice cream with remaining vanilla ice cream and cherries.

9 Place reserved chocolate cake on top of chocolate ice cream, pressing cake down firmly against ice cream. Cover bowl with freezer film; place bowl in freezer until ice cream is firm, at least 4 hours.

10 Prepare Chocolate Bow and Ribbon Streamers.

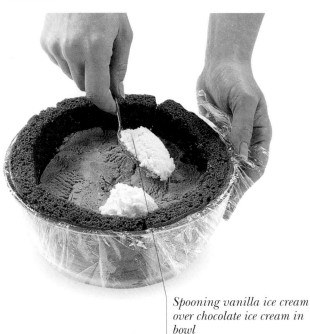

Spooning vanilla ice cream over chocolate ice cream in bowl

11 Heat grill. Evenly sprinkle coconut in baking tray; grill for 3 minutes or until lightly toasted, stirring frequently. Set aside.

12 Prepare butter cream: in medium bowl, with electric mixer, beat icing sugar, butter and *2 teaspoons hot water* until light and fluffy, scraping bowl often with rubber spatula. Beat in vanilla essence until smooth.

13 Remove ice cream cake from freezer. Turn cake out on to chilled freezerproof cake stand or platter; remove cling film. With palette knife, thinly spread butter cream over cake, covering a small area at a time and immediately pressing toasted coconut on to butter cream.

14 Continue until cake is completely covered with butter cream and toasted coconut. Decorate cake with chocolate bow and ribbon streamers. Keep cake in freezer until ready to serve.

TO SERVE
Leave cake to stand at room temperature for 20 minutes for easier slicing.

When Ice Cream Bombe is cut, it reveals its pretty coloured layers of cake, ice cream and cherries

MELON SORBET

6-8 servings

Allow 15 minutes preparation, plus freezing time

1 ripe gallia, charentais or cantaloupe melon (800 g/1 ³/₄ lb)

Juice of ¹/₂ lemon

4 egg whites

100 g/3 ¹/₂ oz caster sugar

1 Remove and discard rind and seeds from melon; cut melon into chunks. In food processor, blend melon chunks and lemon juice until smooth.

2 Turn blended melon and lemon mixture into 1.7 litre/3 pint rigid freezer container and level surface; place in freezer until mixture is just beginning to set round edges.

3 In large bowl, with electric mixer on full speed, beat egg whites until soft peaks form.

4 Into beaten egg whites, gradually sprinkle caster sugar, 1 tablespoon at a time, beating well after each addition until sugar completely dissolves and whites stand in stiff, glossy peaks.

5 Return partially frozen melon mixture to food processor; blend until mixture is broken down. Fold in beaten egg whites until evenly blended. Return melon mixture to rigid container; cover and freeze until firm, about 3 hours.

6 Leave sorbet to stand at room temperature for 10 minutes for easier scooping.

For this attractive presentation, different-sized scoops of sorbet were placed on chilled baking sheet lined with non-stick baking parchment and put in freezer to harden; they were then lifted off and piled on top of each other

Colourful wedges of melon are arranged like spokes of a wheel round edge of serving bowl

RASPBERRY SORBET

8 servings
Allow 20 minutes preparation, plus freezing time

2 x 250 g/8.8 oz packets frozen raspberries

120 g/4 oz caster sugar

1 tablespoon powdered gelatine

4 tablespoons golden syrup, dissolved in 4 tablespoons hot water

5 tablespoons raspberry liqueur

3 tablespoons lemon juice

Kiwi fruit, papaya and fresh raspberries

1 Sprinkle raspberries with sugar; set aside to thaw.

2 In small saucepan, evenly sprinkle gelatine over 250 ml/ 8 fl oz water; allow to stand for 1 minute to soften. Cook over medium heat until gelatine completely dissolves, stirring often. Remove saucepan from heat.

3 Over large bowl, with back of spoon, press and scrape raspberries with their syrup firmly against medium-mesh sieve to purée; discard pips left in sieve.

4 Stir golden syrup, liqueur and lemon juice into raspberry purée, then stir in dissolved gelatine, a little at a time, until well mixed.

5 Pour raspberry mixture into rigid freezer container. Freeze until partially frozen, about 2 hours, stirring occasionally.

6 Transfer partially frozen raspberry mixture to food processor; blend until mixture is broken down. Return mixture to rigid container; cover and freeze until firm, about 3 hours.

7 Arrange some kiwi fruit, papaya and fresh raspberries on individual plates. Place small scoops of sorbet next to fruit.

Adding dissolved gelatine to raspberry mixture

Slices of peeled papaya and kiwi fruit add extra colour to individual servings of sorbet

SERVING SORBET AND ICE CREAM
For an attractive presentation, sorbet and ice cream look best served in scoops. For easy serving, with ice cream scoop, take balls of sorbet or ice cream from container and place on chilled baking sheet lined with non-stick baking parchment.

Immediately place baking sheet in freezer; leave until sorbet or ice cream hardens. To serve, lift scoops off parchment and place on dessert plates or in dishes at last minute.

ITALIAN TARTUFO

6 servings

Allow 2 ³/₄ hours preparation, plus final freezing time

900 ml/1 ¹/₂ pints vanilla ice cream

6 amaretti biscuits

2 tablespoons almond liqueur or orange juice

175 g/6 oz plain chocolate, broken into pieces

45 g/1 ¹/₂ oz butter

1 tablespoon golden syrup

90 g/3 oz walnut pieces, toasted

1 Place ice cream in refrigerator to soften slightly. Chill small baking sheet in freezer.

2 Meanwhile, place amaretti biscuits on plate; pour over almond liqueur or orange juice. Leave to stand until liqueur is absorbed, turning biscuits occasionally.

3 Line chilled baking sheet with non-stick baking parchment. Working quickly, with large ice cream scoop, scoop a ball of ice cream. Gently press an amaretti into centre.

4 Reshape ice cream into ball around amaretti; place on lined baking sheet. Repeat with remaining ice cream and amaretti to make 6 ice cream balls. Freeze until firm, about 1 ¹/₂ hours.

5 In bowl over pan of gently simmering water, heat chocolate pieces, butter and golden syrup, stirring frequently, until melted and smooth. Remove bowl from pan.

6 Remove baking sheet with ice cream balls from freezer.

7 Place 1 ice cream ball on metal spatula over bowl of melted chocolate. With large metal spoon, quickly scoop up melted chocolate and pour over ice cream ball to coat completely.

8 Place chocolate-coated ice cream ball on same baking sheet. Firmly pat some walnuts on to chocolate coating.

9 Repeat with remaining ice cream balls, chocolate mixture and nuts. Freeze until ice cream balls are firm, about 1 hour.

10 If not serving on same day, wrap ice cream balls with foil; return to freezer to use within 1 week.

TO SERVE
Leave ice cream balls to stand at room temperature for about 10 minutes to soften slightly for easier eating.

Toasted walnuts are pressed on to chocolate coating before ice cream ball is frozen, so they will be secure for serving

USEFUL
INFORMATION
AND BASIC
RECIPES
107-125

DESSERTS

The recipes in this book fall into the following categories: mousses and soufflés, custards and creams, meringues, pancakes and crêpes, fruit desserts, cakes and gâteaux, sweet pies, tarts and flans, pastries, and frozen desserts. Within each category the recipes range from simple everyday desserts to classic dishes, and popular recipes calling for slightly more advanced techniques. On these two pages, you will find useful information on general dessert-making techniques.

USING GELATINE

Many desserts, such as mousses and cold soufflés, depend on gelatine to make them set. Gelatine is available as powder or leaf, and the two can be used interchangeably. To substitute leaf gelatine for powder, use 2 leaves for each 7 g/ ¼ oz powdered gelatine (1 tablespoon).

DISSOLVING GELATINE
For properly set, jellied mixtures, gelatine must be dissolved completely in hot liquid such as water, milk or fruit juice in a bowl or saucepan; no visible bits of gelatine should remain in the mixture or they will spoil its clarity and/or smoothness.

Constant stirring is essential to make sure gelatine is completely dissolved.

Gelatine granules that splash up the side of bowl or saucepan are difficult to dissolve, so always stir mixture steadily but not too vigorously.

For best results, powdered gelatine should not be added directly to hot liquid. The granules could lump together and not dissolve completely, and could then spoil the dessert.

Leaf gelatine should always be soaked in water to soften it, then squeezed out before being added to hot liquid.

To check powdered gelatine has dissolved completely: *run rubber spatula through mixture, next to side of pan or bowl, to see if granules are all dissolved*

TURNING OUT GELATINE DESSERTS
Individual desserts set with gelatine can be turned out right on to dessert plates for serving. Turn out large desserts on to serving platter (moisten platter first so that if dessert comes out off-centre on platter, it can be moved easily to centre).

- Fill sink or large basin with warm, not hot, water.

- Carefully loosen edges of dessert from mould with palette knife.

- Dip mould into warm water just to rim for about 10 seconds. Be careful not to melt dessert.

- Lift mould out of water and shake it gently to loosen dessert.

- Invert serving platter on top of mould.

- Quickly invert mould and platter together; gently lift off mould.

ADDING INGREDIENTS TO GELATINE
In most recipes, a gelatine mixture should be partially set before other ingredients are added, or solid ingredients such as sliced fruit might sink to the bottom, and whipped cream could lose its volume by the time it is thoroughly blended in. When solids are to be added, gelatine mixture should have thickened to consistency of unbeaten egg white. This partially thickened stage allows for even distribution of solids. When adding whipped cream, chill mixture slightly longer, until it mounds when dropped from spoon.

If gelatine mixture thickens too much before other ingredients are folded in or it is turned into a mould, place bowl of mixture in hot water and stir occasionally for 1 minute or less to melt gelatine. Then chill mixture again, stirring occasionally.

CHILLING GELATINE DESSERTS
In order to set, a gelatine mixture must be chilled. Stir mixture occasionally while it chills, so that it cools and thickens evenly. For faster thickening, place saucepan or bowl containing mixture in larger bowl of iced water. Stir mixture often until it reaches desired consistency. Or place saucepan or bowl in freezer and stir often until mixture is of desired consistency. Do not leave mixture in freezer until it sets; ice crystals will form and make mixture watery, spoiling the dessert.

To test consistency of gelatine mixture: *take up spoonful of mixture and drop it on top. It should 'mound', not disappear*

EGGS: HANDLE WITH CARE

Raw or undercooked eggs may pose a risk of salmonellosis, food poisoning caused by salmonella bacteria found in some eggs. While this risk is extremely small, it does exist, so it is a good idea to follow some simple rules. When making a custard, be sure that the eggs are cooked and the custard thickened properly, but do not allow the custard to boil or it will curdle. Proper storage and cooking of eggs and handling of egg-rich foods is necessary to prevent growth of potentially harmful bacteria. For safety first, take these precautions.

• Buy only clean, uncracked eggs from a reputable source.

• Don't buy too many eggs at a time; buy only as many as you need.

• When you bring eggs home, put them in the refrigerator as soon as possible.

• Keep eggs in their box, pointed ends downwards.

• Use eggs within 1 week of purchase.

• If a speck of yolk gets into egg whites while separating eggs, use a spoon, not the shell, to remove it. The egg shell might not be clean.

• To test an egg for freshness: place in a bowl of cold water; if it begins to float, it is not fresh.

• Serve eggs and egg-rich foods as soon as they are cooked; or, if you've made them ahead, refrigerate them at once and use within 3 days.

• The following, in particular, are advised not to eat raw or undercooked eggs:
  a) elderly whose immune systems are weakened with age
  b) infants whose immune systems are not yet fully developed
  c) pregnant women
  d) anyone with an immune system weakened by disease or anticancer treatments.

THICKENING WITH EGGS

Many different desserts use eggs as a thickening agent in the form of a custard. The key to successful custards is careful control of heat; too high a heat causes eggs to curdle, resulting in a lumpy, thin mixture. However, it is also important that the heat is high enough (see Eggs: Handle with Care, left).

For successful custards, always use a heavy, non-stick saucepan, or double boiler, and stir mixture constantly with a whisk until it thickens and coats a metal spoon well. Take care not to let mixture boil or it will curdle. Check thickness by lifting spoon from custard and holding it up for 15-20 seconds; if back of spoon does not show through it, custard has thickened to right consistency.

To test consistency of custard: *lift spoon from pan and hold it up for 15-20 seconds; back of spoon should not show through mixture*

HOT SOUFFLÉS

Raised high with beaten egg whites, light, fluffy, hot dessert soufflés need to be carefully timed since they should be served as soon as they are taken from the oven: they tend to collapse if left to stand for more than a few minutes. Both the basic sauce and the soufflé dish itself can be prepared well in advance. Don't open oven door before end of specified baking time; a rush of cold air into the oven could cause soufflé to collapse.

With wire whisk, gradually folding soufflé mixture into egg whites

With back of spoon, making 2.5 cm/1 inch indentation round top of soufflé for 'top hat' effect

MOUSSES

The light, creamy texture of a mousse comes from eggs, custard or whipped cream, or a combination of these, blended into melted chocolate, fruit purée or nuts.

To achieve a smooth, creamy texture, it is essential to fold and blend ingredients in as evenly as possible; for best results, use a wire whisk or rubber spatula when folding in or blending, and a 'figure of eight' action.

SAUCES

A repertoire of sweet sauces enables the cook to put a special finishing touch to a wide variety of desserts. On these pages you will find sauces to enhance the flavour and appeal of fresh, canned and frozen fruits; home-made or bought pastries, flans and cakes; frozen desserts; and bread and rice puddings.

Today's sauces aren't just poured over foods. They can be puddled on the plate or spooned round food to frame it like in a picture. More, sauces themselves can be decorated, with designs piped or stirred in; see Decorating with Sauces (pages 16-17) for ideas to copy or to spark your own imagination.

CHOCOLATE SAUCES

CHOCOLATE CREAM SAUCE

175 g/6 oz plain chocolate, broken into pieces	**1** In bowl over saucepan of gently simmering water, melt pieces of chocolate with golden syrup, stirring. Remove bowl from pan; stir in remaining ingredients.
125 ml/4 fl oz golden syrup	
4 tablespoons single cream	**2** Serve warm over profiteroles or ice cream.
15 g/ 1/2 oz butter	

CHOCOLATE RUM SAUCE

120 g/4 oz plain chocolate, broken into pieces	**1** In non-stick saucepan over medium heat, bring *5 tablespoons water* to the boil with all the other ingredients, stirring. Reduce heat to medium-low; simmer, stirring, until mixture thickens and is smooth, about 3 minutes. Remove from heat; stir in rum.
3 tablespoons caster sugar	
30 g/1 oz butter	
1 tablespoon rum	
	2 Serve warm over bananas, ice cream or poached pears.

CHOCOLATE MARSHMALLOW SAUCE

60 g/2 oz plain chocolate, broken into pieces	**1** In non-stick saucepan over low heat, cook chocolate, marshmallows, cream and honey, stirring, until both chocolate and marshmallows have melted.
100 g/3 1/2 oz marshmallows, cut into small pieces	
5 tablespoons double or whipping cream	**2** Serve hot over bananas or ice cream.
5 tablespoons honey	

CREAM AND CUSTARD SAUCES

CHANTILLY CREAM

300 ml/ 1/2 pint double or whipping cream	**1** In bowl, with whisk, rotary beater or electric mixer, whip cream with sugar and vanilla essence until soft peaks form. (Over-whipping causes cream to curdle and turn to butter.)
1-2 tablespoons caster sugar	
1/2 teaspoon vanilla essence	**2** On hot days, chill bowl and beaters. Serve cream on fruit or nut pies or ice cream sundaes.

Brandy Chantilly Cream
Whip cream with sugar as above until soft peaks form; fold in *2 tablespoons brandy.*

Chocolate Chantilly Cream
Place *2 tablespoons drinking chocolate powder* (or 2 tablespoons caster sugar and 2 tablespoons cocoa powder) in bowl; add 300 ml/ 1/2 pint double or whipping cream. Whip as above.

Coffee Chantilly Cream
Place *2 teaspoons instant coffee powder* and 2 tablespoons caster sugar in bowl; add 300 ml/ 1/2 pint double or whipping cream. Whip as above.

CUSTARD SAUCE

3 tablespoons caster sugar	**1** In heavy non-stick saucepan, combine all ingredients except vanilla essence. Cook over medium heat, stirring, until mixture coats back of spoon well, about 15 minutes (do not boil or custard will curdle).
450 ml/ 3/4 pint milk	
1 egg yolk	
1 tablespoon cornflour	
1/2 teaspoon vanilla essence	**2** Remove from heat; stir in vanilla essence. Chill. Serve with fruit pies and crumbles, fruit tarts and flans and poached or stewed fruit.

EGG CUSTARD SAUCE

4 egg yolks	**1** In heavy non-stick saucepan over low heat, or in double boiler over hot, not boiling, water, with wire whisk, stir egg yolks and sugar.
5 tablespoons caster sugar	
450 ml/ ³/₄ pint milk	
1 teaspoon vanilla essence	**2** Gradually add milk and cook, stirring, until mixture thickens and coats back of spoon well, about 25 minutes (do not boil or custard will curdle). Stir in vanilla essence. Serve warm or cold with apple or other fruit pies, or with poached or stewed fruit.

SUGAR SAUCES

BUTTERSCOTCH SAUCE

225 g/8 oz light soft brown sugar	**1** In non-stick saucepan over medium heat, heat brown sugar, single cream, butter and golden syrup just to boiling point, stirring occasionally.
125 ml/4 fl oz single cream	
30 g/1 oz butter	
2 tablespoons golden syrup	**2** Serve warm over vanilla or rum and raisin ice cream, or with baked custard.

HOT FUDGE SAUCE

300 g/10 oz caster sugar	**1** In non-stick saucepan over medium heat, bring first 4 ingredients to the boil, stirring constantly. Set sugar thermo-meter in place and continue boiling, stirring occasionally, until temperature reaches 109°C/228°F or until small amount of mixture dropped from tip of spoon back into mixture spins 5 mm/¹/₄ inch thread.
125 ml/4 fl oz milk	
5 tablespoons golden syrup	
60 g/2 oz plain chocolate, broken into pieces	
15 g/ ¹/₂ oz butter	
1 teaspoon vanilla essence	**2** Remove from heat; stir in butter and vanilla essence. Serve hot over vanilla ice cream or poached pears.

CARAMEL SAUCE

30 g/1 oz butter	**1** In medium saucepan over medium heat, melt butter; stir in flour.
2 tablespoons plain flour	
450 ml/ ³/₄ pint single cream	**2** Gradually stir in cream; cook, stirring constantly, until mixture thickens.
165 g/5 ¹/₂ oz light soft brown sugar	
150 g/5 oz caster sugar	**3** Stir in brown and caster sugars. Serve warm or cover and refri-gerate to serve cold; serve over baked bananas or apples, or vanilla or chocolate ice cream.

PRALINE SAUCE

225 g/8 oz light soft brown sugar	**1** In small saucepan over me-dium heat, stir all ingredients, except nuts, with *2 tablespoons water* until sugar dissolves. Stir in nuts.
125 ml/4 fl oz golden syrup	
15 g/ ¹/₂ oz butter	**2** Serve hot over rice pudding, ice cream or waffles.
60 g/2 oz shelled pecan or walnut pieces, finely chopped	

BRANDY BUTTER

120 g/4 oz icing sugar, sifted	**1** In medium bowl, with electric mixer, beat icing sugar with butter until creamy; beat in brandy.
90 g/3 oz butter, softened	
2 tablespoons brandy	**2** Spoon into small bowl and refrigerate if not serving immedi-ately. Serve with hot mince pies or Christmas pudding.

Deluxe Brandy Butter
Prepare as above; fold in *4 tablespoons double or whipping cream, whipped*, after brandy.

Rum Butter
Prepare as for Brandy Butter, but using *rum* instead of brandy.

FRUIT SAUCES

BLACKBERRY SAUCE

600 g/1 ¼ lb fresh or frozen blackberries

120 g/4 oz caster sugar

2 tablespoons lemon juice

1 In medium saucepan over medium heat, heat berries, sugar and lemon juice, stirring occasionally, until hot and bubbly. Work through sieve. Cover; chill.

2 Serve over ice cream and other fruits.

CHERRY SAUCE

450 g/1 lb cherries, stoned

4 tablespoons caster sugar

1 In medium saucepan over medium heat, in *150 ml/ ¼ pint water*, bring cherries to the boil.

2 Reduce heat to low; cover pan and simmer cherries for about 5 minutes or until tender.

3 During last minute of cooking, add sugar. Serve hot, poured over pancakes; or serve cold over ice cream or creamy puddings.

PEACH SAUCE

1 x 400 g/14 oz can peaches in natural juice

¼ teaspoon almond essence

1 In food processor or blender, blend ingredients together until smooth.

2 Serve over ice cream.

RASPBERRY SAUCE

300 g/10 oz raspberries

1 tablespoon caster sugar

1 In food processor or blender, blend raspberries and sugar until smooth, adding *a little water* if needed to thin sauce.

2 Press sauce through fine sieve with wooden spoon to remove pips. Serve with peaches or strawberries, or over ice cream.

COMPOTE SAUCE

3 large nectarines

3 large plums

125 ml/4 fl oz orange juice

100 g/3 ½ oz caster sugar

2 tablespoons brandy

1 Cut fruit into wedges, discarding stones.

2 In medium saucepan over low heat, cook fruit and juice for 10 minutes or until tender, stirring occasionally. Remove from heat.

3 Add sugar and brandy; stir until sugar is dissolved. Serve over vanilla ice cream.

MAPLE AND ORANGE SAUCE

1 x 325 g/11 oz can mandarin orange segments, drained and chopped

175 ml/6 fl oz maple syrup

30 g/1 oz butter

1 In medium saucepan over low heat, heat all ingredients until hot and butter melts.

2 Serve warm over pancakes, French toast or ice cream sundaes.

MELBA SAUCE

75 g/2 ½ oz redcurrant jelly

300 g/10 oz raspberries

30 g/1 oz icing sugar, sifted

Juice of 1 lemon

1 In small saucepan over low heat, heat redcurrant jelly until melted.

2 In food processor, blend raspberries, melted redcurrant jelly, icing sugar and lemon juice until smooth. Press through sieve.

3 Serve over ice cream or poached peaches or pears.

ORANGE SAUCE

60 g/2 oz butter

175 g/6 oz icing sugar, sifted

5 tablespoons orange juice

2 tablespoons grated orange zest

1 In small saucepan over low heat, melt butter. Stir in icing sugar, orange juice and orange zest.

2 Cook over low heat, stirring frequently, until heated through. Serve over pancakes.

CAKES

The cake recipes in this book generally follow one of two basic methods. Most contain butter or soft margarine and are mixed and beaten in one bowl. Others, such as sponges and Swiss rolls, have beaten egg whites folded in at the end to give them a light and fluffy texture. Whichever type you bake, if you follow the directions given here you can be assured of success every time.

Before you start, read the recipe carefully and assemble all ingredients and equipment. Prepare tins, put oven racks in correct position, and preheat oven if necessary.

BEFORE YOU START

INGREDIENTS
In the recipes in this book medium-sized eggs are used. Don't be tempted to substitute different ingredients for the ones in the recipe; they will give different results.

MEASURING
Weigh and measure dry and liquid ingredients carefully. Spoon measures used in the recipes are metric spoons (1 tablespoon = 15 ml and 1 teaspoon = 5 ml). All spoon measures of dry ingredients are level.

TINS
Use shiny metal tins or tins with non-stick finish. Avoid old-fashioned tins with insulated bases. If using glass or porcelain-coated aluminium tins with a non-stick finish, reduce oven temperature by 10°C/25°F. Cake tins are available in round, square or rectangular shapes. Be sure your tins are the size and shape called for in the recipe. Measure the top inside of a tin for length, width or diameter; measure perpendicular inside for depth. Prepare tins according to recipe instructions (see How to Grease and Line Tins, page 114).

Springform tin: *has side section which can be removed without disturbing contents*

Angel cake or tube tin: *has centre tube; may or may not have removable bottom*

Swiss roll tin: *shallow rectangular tin, usually 2.5 cm/1 inch deep*

German Bundt or kugelhopf mould: *fluted, with centre tube; for elegant cakes and desserts*

STORING AND FREEZING CAKES

Storing
Sandwich cakes and ring cakes filled and/or iced with butter cream or glacé icing should be kept under an inverted bowl or tin to protect icing; store cakes filled and/or iced with butter cream in a cool place or the refrigerator, to prevent butter from becoming rancid.

Cakes covered with whipped cream or soft cheese icing, or those that have any sort of cream filling, should be kept refrigerated and are best eaten within 1-2 days.

Wrap rich fruit cakes closely and store in airtight containers in cool place; they will improve with storage. For very rich cakes, before storing, sprinkle cake with wine or brandy, or wrap in wine- or brandy-dampened cloth, then overwrap and store in airtight container for up to 2 months. Re-dampen cloth weekly with more wine or brandy, if you like. Ice or decorate cake just before serving.

Freezing
Cakes in the freezer make wonderful standby desserts. For freezer storage, all cakes must be wrapped or packaged in materials specifically designed for freezer use. Wrapping materials for foods must be moisture-proof: use heavy-duty freezer foil, freezer paper or freezer wrap. Secure packages with freezer or masking tape. Use waterproof felt-tip pens or markers for writing on labels, freezer tape or freezer paper.

Un-iced cakes should be closely wrapped in freezer paper, freezer wrap or foil, and securely sealed with tape.

Most cakes will keep in the freezer for 4-6 months, fruit cakes for up to 12 months.

Open freeze cakes iced and/or piped with butter cream or whipped cream on tray or sheet of card covered with foil until icing hardens, then place frozen cake in rigid container, seal and return to freezer. Iced cakes can be stored in the freezer for 2-3 months.

Do not freeze cakes which have either jam or fruit fillings; they can become soggy when thawed.

Never freeze uncooked cake mixture or cakes with fillings made with cornflour or flour.

Thaw un-iced cakes and fruit cakes in their freezer wrappings at room temperature. Un-iced cakes take about 1 hour to thaw, fruit cakes, 2-3 hours.

Cakes with butter cream and whipped cream icings should be carefully unpacked before they are thawed and placed on their serving plate so that their decoration will not be spoiled. Thaw in refrigerator for 3-4 hours and keep refrigerated until serving time. Be sure to cover and refrigerate leftovers.

MEASURING TINS

Be sure your tins are the kind and size specified in recipe. Measure top inside for length, width or diameter; measure perpendicular inside for depth.

HOW TO GREASE AND LINE TINS

Make sure tins are size called for in recipe, and prepare them before you start mixing cake ingredients. Prepare tins according to instructions in individual recipes.

If tins are to be greased and floured, grease both bottom and sides with softened butter or margarine, using brush, crumpled greaseproof paper or kitchen paper. You can also grease tins with melted butter or margarine using pastry brush to grease evenly. Sprinkle tin with a little flour or, for dark-coloured cakes, with sifted cocoa powder so cake does not have white coating. Shake tin until coated, then invert it and tap to remove excess flour or cocoa. For fruit cakes, grease tins well, line with foil, then grease foil. Some recipes call for bottoms of tins to be lined with baking parchment; grease tin first, then parchment will stick to bottom.

Greasing tin: using brush, crumpled greaseproof paper or kitchen paper, spread tins evenly with melted butter or margarine

Lining tin: where specified, line bottom of greased tin with non-stick baking parchment

Flouring tin: in some recipes, tins are floured after greasing. Sprinkle with flour and shake and turn tin until evenly coated; knock out surplus

HOW TO BEAT MIXTURE

When preparing cake mixture, beat it with electric mixer for length of time specified in recipe. During beating, scrape bowl frequently with rubber spatula so that all cake ingredients are well mixed together. If you use a wooden spoon instead of mixer, you will need to give ingredients a very good beating until mixture is smooth and ingredients are blended thoroughly. Before adding large fruits and nuts to mixture, toss them in about 1 tablespoon of the measured flour, so that they do not sink in mixture.

To beat mixture: beat with electric mixer for specified time, constantly scraping sides of bowl with rubber spatula to make sure ingredients are well mixed in

HOW TO FOLD IN

For cakes made with egg whites, beat egg whites into stiff peaks in bowl. In separate bowl, beat remaining ingredients according to recipe instructions. Using rubber spatula, gently fold egg whites into beaten mixture, cutting down through centre, across bottom and up side of bowl. Give bowl a quarter turn and repeat until mixture is uniformly blended, but do not overfold or egg whites will break down.

To fold mixture: use rubber spatula to fold egg whites into beaten ingredients

FILLING TINS

Pour mixture into prepared tin and tap tin sharply on work surface or cut through it several times with rubber spatula or knife to break any large air bubbles. Spread evenly with spatula.

For mixtures containing beaten egg white, push mixture into tin with rubber spatula. Smooth and level it very lightly, then cut through it with rubber spatula to break any large air bubbles.

To fill tin: with rubber spatula, push mixture into tin, then smooth and level it very lightly

BASIC SANDWICH CAKE RECIPES

The cake recipes on this page provide a good basis for making a variety of different desserts at short notice. Sandwiched together with jam, lemon curd or fresh fruit and whipped cream – nothing could be more simple. The ingredients are carefully balanced, so follow instructions exactly for successful results every time.

VICTORIA SANDWICH

Made by the all-in-one method, this cake is a great stand-by for quick-and-easy desserts and party cakes.

175 g/6 oz soft margarine	**1** Preheat oven to 180°C/350°F/gas 4.
175 g/ 6 oz caster sugar	
3 eggs, beaten	**2** Grease bottoms of two 18 cm/7 inch straight-sided sandwich tins; line with non-stick baking parchment.
175 g/ 6 oz self-raising flour	
1 rounded teaspoon baking powder	

3 In large bowl, beat margarine, sugar, eggs, flour and baking powder for about 2 minutes or until mixture is smooth and all ingredients are thoroughly blended.

4 Divide mixture evenly between prepared tins and smooth tops. Bake for 25-30 minutes or until cake is pale golden and centre springs back when lightly pressed with finger.

5 Turn cakes out on to wire rack. Carefully peel off baking parchment; leave cakes to cool.

Orange or Lemon Sandwich
To creamed mixture, add *finely grated zest of 1 orange or lemon.*

Chocolate Sandwich
In large bowl, blend *1 rounded tablespoon cocoa powder* with *2 tablespoons hot water.* Cool; add remaining cake ingredients and proceed as above.

Coffee Sandwich
Dissolve *1 heaped teaspoon instant coffee powder* in beaten eggs before adding to mixture.

WHISKED SPONGE

4 eggs	**1** Preheat oven to 190°C/[gas 5. Grease bottoms of tw[20 cm/8 inch straight-sided sandwich tins; line with non-stick baking parchment.
120 g/4 oz caster sugar	
120 g/4 oz self-raising flour	

2 Put eggs and sugar in large bowl; beat with electric mixer until mixture is thick, white and creamy and leaves a thick ribbon trail. Sift in flour; carefully fold in with large metal spoon.

3 Divide mixture between tins. Bake for 20 minutes or until centres spring back when lightly pressed. Turn cakes out on to wire rack. Peel off parchment; leave cakes to cool.

CHOCOLATE CAKE

2 eggs	**1** Preheat oven to 170°C/325°F/gas 3. Grease bottoms of two 20 cm/8 inch straight-sided sandwich tins; line with non-stick baking parchment.
150 ml/ ¼ pint sunflower oil	
150 ml/ ¼ pint milk	
2 tablespoons golden syrup	
150 g/5 oz caster sugar	**2** Break eggs into large bowl; add all other ingredients. Beat well for about 2 minutes or until mixture is smooth and all ingredients are thoroughly blended.
190 g/6 ½ oz self-raising flour	
30 g/1 oz cocoa powder, sifted	
1 teaspoon baking powder	**3** Divide mixture between tins. Bake for 30-35 minutes or until cakes shrink away slightly from sides of tins and wooden cocktail stick inserted in centres comes out clean.
1 teaspoon bicarbonate of soda	

4 Turn cakes out on to wire rack; cool, then peel off parchment.

When using electric mixer, occasionally scrape side of bowl with rubber spatula

To test if cake is done, insert wooden cocktail stick in centre – it should come out clean

ICINGS AND FROSTINGS

Most uncooked icings such as butter cream can be made in advance and stored until needed in a tightly covered container to prevent a crust forming on top. If they are refrigerated and become too firm to spread easily, leave them to stand at room temperature, or stir well to soften to spreading consistency.

Allow your cake to cool completely before icing or filling. Trim off any crisp edges with knife or kitchen scissors and brush away all loose crumbs. Keep cake plate clean by covering edges with strips of greaseproof paper. Lay cake on paper strips, placing it in centre of plate. After icing cake, carefully slide out paper strips. Cakes iced with soft cheese, soured cream or whipped cream icings should be refrigerated until served.

Recipes on this and the following page make enough to ice a 33 x 23 cm/13 x 9 inch cake or fill and ice a 20-23 cm/8-9 inch sandwich cake.

To ice cake: cover plate edges with strips of greaseproof paper; lay cake on strips

After icing, carefully slide out strips; if necessary, touch up base with icing

WHIPPED CREAM 'ICING'

450 ml/ ³/₄ pint double or whipping cream

30 g/1 oz icing sugar, sifted

1 teaspoon vanilla essence (optional)

In small bowl, with whisk or electric mixer, whip double or whipping cream with sugar until stiff peaks form; fold in vanilla essence, if you like. Keep iced cake refrigerated until ready to serve.

TECHNIQUES

Sandwich cake
Place one layer of cake, top side down, on serving plate. Cover this layer with either filling or icing, spreading it almost to edge. If filling is soft, spread it only to within 2.5 cm/1 inch of edge. Place second cake layer, top side up, on filling, so that flat bases of two layers face each other, keeping top layer from cracking or sliding off. Ice sides of cake thinly to set any loose crumbs, then apply second, more generous layer of icing, swirling it up to make 1 cm/¹/₂ inch ridge above rim of cake. Finally, ice top of cake, swirling icing or leaving it smooth, as you like. Decorate iced cake if desired.

Oblong cake
Ice top and sides of cake as for sandwich cake, or leave cake in tin and just ice top.

Tube or ring cake
Ice sides, then top and inside centre of cake as for sandwich cake.

Cup cakes
Dip top of each cake in icing, turning it slightly to coat evenly.

Glazing
Brush crumbs from top of cake. Spoon or pour glaze on to top of cake, letting it drip down sides. Spread thicker glazes over top and sides of cake with palette knife.

Drizzling
To make decorative pattern, pour thin icing or glaze from spoon, quickly waving spoon back and forth over cake.

Chocolate Whipped Cream 'Icing'
Prepare as left; fold in *2 tablespoons drinking chocolate powder*, instead of vanilla essence.

Coffee Whipped Cream 'Icing'
Prepare as left; add *1 teaspoon instant coffee powder* with sugar and omit vanilla essence.

Orange Whipped Cream 'Icing'
Prepare as left; add *1 teaspoon grated orange zest* and *¹/₂ teaspoon orange flower water* instead of vanilla essence.

Peppermint Whipped Cream 'Icing'
Whip cream as left; fold in *4 tablespoons crushed peppermints* or *seaside rock* and omit vanilla essence.

BUTTER CREAM

450 g/1 lb icing sugar, sifted

300 g/10 oz butter, softened

A little milk

In large bowl, with electric mixer (or spoon), beat icing sugar and butter until smooth, adding a little milk if necessary until butter cream is smooth with an easy spreading consistency.

Lemon Butter Cream
Prepare as for Butter Cream, but substitute *lemon juice* for milk.

Mocha Butter Cream
Prepare as for Butter Cream, but add *45 g/1½ oz cocoa powder*; substitute *cold black coffee* for milk.

CHOCOLATE SOURED CREAM ICING

175 g/6 oz plain chocolate, broken into pieces

15 g/½ oz butter

150 ml/¼ pint soured cream

30 g/1 oz icing sugar, sifted

1 In bowl over saucepan of gently simmering water, heat chocolate and butter until melted and smooth, stirring occasionally. Remove bowl from pan.

2 In medium bowl, with electric mixer, beat melted chocolate mixture, soured cream and icing sugar until smooth.

SOFT CHEESE ICING

175 g/6 oz full-fat soft cheese, softened

2 tablespoons milk

225 g/8 oz icing sugar, sifted

1½ teaspoons vanilla essence

1 In small bowl, with electric mixer, beat soft cheese and milk just until smooth.

2 Beat in icing sugar and vanilla essence until blended.

Coffee Soft Cheese Icing
Prepare as for Soft Cheese Icing, but add *4 teaspoons instant coffee powder* with icing sugar; omit vanilla essence.

COFFEE FUDGE ICING

90 g/3 oz butter

225 g/8 oz icing sugar, sifted

1 tablespoon milk

1 tablespoon coffee essence

60 g/2 oz walnut pieces, pecans or hazelnuts, finely chopped

Walnut or pecan halves, or shelled whole hazelnuts for decoration

1 In medium bowl, put butter, sifted icing sugar, milk and coffee essence.

2 With electric mixer or spoon, beat ingredients until smooth and with an easy spreading consistency.

3 To icing, add finely chopped walnuts, pecans or hazelnuts; fold in until evenly distributed.

4 After spreading icing on cake, immediately press walnut or pecan halves or shelled whole hazelnuts into icing, around edge of cake or in attractive design over top. Leave to set before serving cake.

DARK CHOCOLATE ICING

175 g/6 oz plain chocolate, broken into pieces

30 g/1 oz butter

2 tablespoons golden syrup

3 tablespoons milk

1 In heavy non-stick saucepan over low heat, or in double boiler over hot, not boiling, water, heat chocolate and butter until melted and completely smooth, stirring occasionally. Remove from heat.

2 With wire whisk or fork, beat in golden syrup and milk until mixture is smooth. Spread while icing is still warm.

MOCHA ICING

350 g/12 oz icing sugar

4 tablespoons cocoa powder

1 teaspoon instant coffee powder

1½ teaspoons vanilla essence

1 Into large bowl, sift icing sugar, cocoa and coffee powders; stir well to mix.

2 Gradually add *about 3 tablespoons warm water*, mixing until icing has a coating consistency; stir in vanilla essence.

CHOCOLATE ICING

350 g/12 oz icing sugar

2 tablespoons cocoa powder

1 Into large bowl, sift icing sugar and cocoa powder.

2 Gradually add *about 3 tablespoons warm water*, mixing until icing has a coating consistency.

GLAZES

These recipes make enough for a 33 x 23 cm/ 13 x 9 inch or a 20-23 cm/8-9 inch round cake.

LEMON GLAZE

175 g/ 6 oz caster sugar	**1** In bowl, mix sugar and lemon juice until sugar dissolves.
Juice of 1 1/2 lemons	

2 With back of spoon, spread glaze over warm plain cake. Heat of cake causes lemon juice to run, giving cake a lovely lemon flavour and making it moist; sugar remains on top as a shiny crust.

RICH CHOCOLATE GLAZE

275 g/9 oz plain chocolate, broken into pieces	**1** In bowl over saucepan of gently simmering water, heat all ingredients until chocolate melts and mixture is smooth, stirring constantly.
2 tablespoons icing sugar, sifted	
3 tablespoons orange liquer	**2** Remove bowl from pan. Leave glaze to stand at room temperature to cool slightly until of spreading consistency, then spread while still warm.
3 tablespoons milk	
1 teaspoon instant coffee powder	

Spreading chocolate glaze over cake: *stand cake on wire rack over sheet of greaseproof paper; spread glaze over top and sides with palette knife, letting excess glaze drip on to paper*

DECORATIVE TOUCHES

It is easy to add decorative touches to cakes that are covered in icing. To make spiral patterns below left, place cake on a turntable if you have one.

Press tip of palette knife into centre – turn cake, slowly moving knife outwards

Draw prongs of fork across icing in parallel rows; repeat rows at right angles

GLACÉ ICINGS

You only need a very small amount of glacé icing to make a plain cake look special.

GLACÉ ICING

60 g/2 oz icing sugar	**1** Into bowl, sift icing sugar.
Food colouring (optional)	**2** Gradually add about *1 1/2 teaspoons warm water*, beating vigorously until icing reaches a coating consistency. Beat in a few drops of food colouring, if you like.

Coffee Glacé Icing
Prepare as for Glacé Icing, but substitute *1 teaspoon coffee essence* for the same amount of water.

Lemon Glacé Icing
Prepare as for Glacé Icing, but substitute *lemon juice* for water; use *yellow food colouring*, if you like.

Liqueur Glacé Icing
Prepare as for Glacé Icing, but use *liqueur of your choice* instead of water.

Orange Glacé Icing
Prepare as for Glacé Icing, but substitute *orange juice* for water; use *orange food colouring*, if you like.

TOPPINGS

Each of the following recipes makes enough to spread on top of a 33 x 23 cm/13 x 9 inch cake.

NUTTY FUDGE TOPPING

250 ml/8 fl oz double or whipping cream

100 g/3 ¹/₂ oz caster sugar

30 g/1 oz butter

1 tablespoon golden syrup

120 g/4 oz plain chocolate, broken into pieces

200 g/7 oz shelled nuts, finely chopped

1 In non-stick saucepan over medium-high heat, bring first 5 ingredients to the boil, stirring constantly.

2 Reduce heat to medium and cook for 5 minutes, stirring constantly. Remove pan from heat. Cool slightly, about 10 minutes, then stir in nuts.

3 Quickly pour topping evenly over cake, allowing some to run down sides. Refrigerate until topping is firm, about 1 hour.

PRALINE AND COCONUT TOPPING

120 g/4 oz butter

100 g/3 ¹/₂ oz desiccated coconut

90 g/3 oz shelled nuts, finely chopped

165 g/5 ¹/₂ oz soft brown sugar

1 Start to prepare topping about 10 minutes before end of cake's baking time. In medium saucepan over low heat, melt butter.

2 Stir in coconut, chopped nuts and sugar. Remove saucepan from heat.

3 When cake is done, spread coconut mixture over hot cake. Grill cake for 2 minutes or until golden.

CRACKED CARAMEL

60 g/2 oz sugar

1 In small heavy saucepan over medium heat, heat sugar until melted and a light brown colour (about 6 minutes), stirring constantly.

2 Immediately pour caramel on to greased baking sheet; cool.

3 With rolling pin, crack caramel. If not using immediately, store in tightly covered container.

FILLINGS

Each of the following recipes makes enough filling for a 20-23 cm/8-9 inch sandwich cake.

ALMOND FILLING

120 g/4 oz blanched almonds, toasted

120 g/4 oz icing sugar, sifted

60 g/2 oz butter, softened

About 2 tablespoons orange juice or orange liqueur

1 In food processor, finely grind toasted almonds.

2 In bowl, mix ground almonds with remaining ingredients until evenly blended, adding enough orange juice or liqueur to reach an easy spreading consistency.

VANILLA CUSTARD FILLING

450 ml/ ³/₄ pint milk

50 g/1 ²/₃ oz caster sugar

25 g/ ³/₄ oz cornflour

2 egg yolks

1 teaspoon vanilla essence

1 In non-stick saucepan, stir together all ingredients except vanilla essence.

2 Over medium-low heat, cook until mixture thickens and coats back of spoon well, about 20 minutes (do not boil or mixture will curdle). Stir in vanilla essence. Cool, then chill for 30 minutes.

FRESH LEMON FILLING

1 tablespoon grated lemon zest

4 tablespoons lemon juice

50 g/1 ²/₃ oz caster sugar

4 teaspoons cornflour

15 g/ ¹/₂ oz butter

1 In small saucepan over medium heat, stir all ingredients except butter with *125 ml/4 fl oz water* until well blended. Cook until mixture thickens and boils, stirring.

2 Reduce heat; simmer for 1 minute, stirring occasionally. Remove from heat; stir in butter. Allow mixture to cool at room temperature.

Fresh Orange Filling
Prepare as for Fresh Lemon Filling, but substitute *orange zest and juice* for lemon zest and juice.

PASTRY-MAKING

You can make your own 'designer' pies, tarts and flans with the recipes and ideas on these pages. Pick a pastry to make the crust for any type of pie, whether served hot or cold; or choose a crumb crust to hold chilled fillings prepared separately. (An unbaked crumb crust, incidentally, is the quickest pie shell you can make.) The basic pastries for sweet pies are on pages 64-65; for tarts, flans and tartlets on page 77. These can be filled with fruit, custard, ice cream or mousse and then given the decorative touches – edges, tops, decorations, arrangements – that make a pie, tart or flan your very own creation. If you take a short cut and use bought frozen pastry, follow the same techniques for rolling and using the dough in double or single crust pies and tarts and flans.

EQUIPMENT

Using the right utensils can help make pastry-making easy and quick. Here are some of the most useful items. The pastry blender is a very clever invention, available at most good kitchenware shops; it is an excellent tool for cutting fat into flour.

Rolling pin: choose the widest possible pin for easy rolling out of dough

Pastry scraper: use for scraping off any dough that sticks to work surface

Pastry wheel: straight or ripple-edged wheel with handle, which speeds cutting of pastry dough

Pastry blender: for cutting fats evenly into dry ingredients

Pastry brush: for brushing on egg and milk glazes, or jam glaze on fruit flans

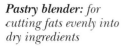

PASTRY-MAKING TECHNIQUES

ROLLING OUT DOUGH

Dough should be rolled with floured rolling pin on lightly floured surface. Slightly flatten ball of dough and roll it out, moving from centre to edge, keeping it circular. Push sides in occasionally by hand, if necessary, and lift rolling pin slightly as you near edge to avoid making dough too thin. Lift dough occasionally to ensure that it is not sticking. If it does stick, loosen it with pastry scraper and sprinkle more flour on surface underneath. Mend any cracks in dough as they appear, patching with dough cut from edge. Moisten torn edges, lay patch over tear and press it into position.

Rolling out dough: roll dough from centre to edge, keeping it circular. Push sides in occasionally by hand, if necessary, and lift rolling pin slightly as you near edge to avoid making dough too thin

LINING PIE DISHES AND TINS

If you are making a double crust pie, divide dough into 2 pieces, 1 slightly larger than the other. Use larger piece for lining pie dish or tin.

Roll out dough into round about 3 mm/$\frac{1}{8}$ inch thick and 4 cm/1 $\frac{1}{2}$ inches larger all round than upside-down pie dish or tin. Roll dough loosely round rolling pin and lift on to dish. Unroll and ease into dish, pressing on to bottom and up side with fingertips. Do not stretch dough; it will shrink back while baking. Make Decorative Pastry Edge (pages 66-67) and fill pie, or make top crust if it is a double crust pie.

PIE DISHES

Be sure your pie dish or tin is size specified in recipe. To check size, if it has not been marked on pie dish or tin by manufacturer, use a ruler to measure dish or tin from inside edge to inside edge.

Pie dishes of the same diameter may differ in capacity; the recipes in this book are for shallow pie dishes.

For nicely browned pastry top and bottom, use metal such as anodized aluminium, tin or enamel pie dishes and tins.

Don't grease pie dishes or tins unless recipe says to do so. Most pastry contains enough fat to keep it from sticking to pie dish or tin.

BAKING BLIND

A pie, tart or flan shell may be baked blind, that is, baked first without a filling. If it is to be filled with a very juicy filling, it should not be pricked with a fork before baking. Instead, after lining the pie dish or tin with dough and making a decorative edge, cut a sheet of foil and place it in the pie shell, pressing it gently on to the bottom and side. Then, according to recipe instructions, half fill the foil-lined shell with dried or baking beans or uncooked rice. Bake in preheated 220°C/425°F/gas 7 oven for 10 minutes; carefully remove foil, with beans or rice if used, and continue baking pie shell until golden. Cool pie shell completely before filling. Dried and baking beans and rice can be stored, after cooling, in covered container and used time and again for baking blind; do not use in cooking.

Half filling foil liner with dried beans for baking blind

A BAKING PRECAUTION

Sometimes, despite the cook's best efforts, juices from very ripe fruit will bubble over the rim of the pie dish on to the oven floor. If you are using very juicy fruit and suspect that this might happen, tear off a 30 cm/12 inch square of foil and turn the edges up 1 cm/1/2 inch on all sides; place on another oven rack directly below the pie to catch any dripping juices, and bake the pie as directed. Even if the pie does bubble over, the foil should catch all the drips and save on oven cleaning.

GLAZING AND BAKING

For a golden glaze, brush top crust (not edge) with milk, undiluted evaporated milk, or lightly beaten egg white; sprinkle crust with sugar, if you like. If pie crust edges begin to brown too much during baking, cover them with strips of foil to prevent burning. If top crust seems to be browning too much, cover pie loosely with foil for the last 15 minutes of baking time.

Covering pie crust edges with strips of foil to prevent burning

FREEZING PASTRY

Uncooked Pastry Dough

Roll out pastry dough into rounds 4 cm/1 1/2 inches larger all round than upside-down pie dishes or tins, stack with 2 sheets of greaseproof paper between each, wrap and freeze. Use within 2-3 months.

To use, place round of dough on pie dish or tin; thaw for 10-15 minutes before shaping.

Pie Crusts

Freeze baked or unbaked shells in their dishes or tins, or in reusable foil pie tins. Store baked shells for 4-6 months; thaw, unwrapped, at room temperature for 15 minutes. Store unbaked shells for 2-3 months.

To use, prick unfilled shells well with fork and bake, without thawing, for about 20 minutes in preheated 220°C/425°F/gas 7 oven; or fill and bake as instructed in individual recipes.

Fruit Pies and Tarts

Freeze baked or unbaked fruit pies for 2-3 months. To freeze unbaked fruit pies, if fruit is very juicy, add 1-2 tablespoons extra flour or cornflour to filling. Do not cut slits in top crust. Wrap and freeze. Or, if pie is fragile, first open freeze until firm, then cover top with paper plate for protection, wrap and return to freezer.

To cook unbaked fruit pie, unwrap, cut slits in top crust and bake in preheated oven from frozen, allowing 15-20 minutes additional baking time or until fruit is hot and bubbling.

Thaw baked pies, unwrapped, at room temperature for about 30 minutes, then bake in preheated 180°C/350°F/gas 4 oven for 30 minutes or until warm.

Frozen Fillings

Pies with ice cream or frozen fillings will not only be easier to cut when serving, but also have more flavour, if they are allowed to stand at room temperature for about 15 minutes after removal from freezer. Unwrap them first so that any decoration will not be spoiled.

STORING PASTRY

Most fruit pies and flans can be kept at room temperature overnight, even in warm weather, covered with foil once cold. For longer storage (2 or 3 days), refrigerate; then freshen by warming them in oven.

Pies and tarts with cream, custard, whipped cream or soft cheese filling or fillings set with gelatine should be refrigerated and used within a day or so.

Balls of unbaked pastry dough may be wrapped in either greaseproof paper or foil, and stored in the refrigerator for a day or two.

HINTS AND TIPS

Here you'll find some do's and don'ts of good cooking, selected to help you make the recipes in this book with the least time and effort, and the greatest of ease. One very important rule should be observed with every single recipe: before you start to cook, read the recipe through to make sure you understand the instructions; then assemble ingredients and equipment to make sure you have everything you need.

Finally, treat your book as a 'working manual'; keep a pencil at the side and if you find a cake takes 20 minutes to cook in your oven rather than the recommended 30 minutes, jot this down by the recipe, together with any other useful comments – for example, which dish you used, whether you added pecans rather than walnuts, and so on.

GENERAL HINTS

• When recipe calls for butter or margarine, it refers to solid, block form. When cake recipe calls for soft margarine, use the soft tub variety (it has air beaten in). Don't use low-fat margarines and vegetable oil spreads, which contain more water and less fat; they may give different results.

• Brown sugar stored in freezer will be soft and usable when thawed. If brown sugar sticks together in lumps, soften in the microwave for a short time.

• When softened butter or margarine is needed in a hurry, cut the amount called for into small pieces; it will soften more quickly at room temperature than a large piece.

• Dry ingredients – flour, sugar, baking powder, bicarbonate of soda – should be kept in airtight containers in a cool, dry place.

• To cut sticky foods like candied peel, glacé cherries or dates, keep dipping knife or scissors in flour.

• When measuring ingredients to add to those already in mixing bowl, never hold a measuring spoon over the bowl. One slip of the hand and the recipe could be ruined by too much vanilla essence, baking powder or whatever.

• Place a folded damp tea towel or dish cloth under bowl when mixing by hand or folding ingredients into a mixture; bowl won't slip while mixing.

• To determine volume of mould, simply measure amount of water it takes to fill it to the brim.

• Use the right knife and cutting techniques, and slices will be perfect when you cut cakes and desserts.
For sandwich and layer cakes, use a well-sharpened chef's knife.
For meringue desserts and Swiss rolls, use a knife with a thin, sharp blade and wipe it with a damp cloth or kitchen paper after every cut.
Before cutting cheesecakes, mousse cakes and other 'sticky' desserts, dip knife blade in very hot water and dry quickly with kitchen paper. The heated blade will cut through without sticking.
In all cases, use a sawing motion and a light touch to avoid crushing the cake or dessert out of shape.

• If you have leftover whipped cream, pipe it or drop it by heaping spoonfuls on to a baking sheet and freeze. When cream is firm, loosen with a palette knife and store in polythene bag in freezer. To use, place frozen piped shapes or dollops on top of desserts; they will thaw in just a few minutes.

CUSTARDS AND CREAMS

• Stirring a little hot liquid into beaten eggs heats eggs so they will not curdle when added to more hot liquid.

• Always remove a custard mixture from the heat when checking to see if it is thick enough. Even just a few seconds extra cooking time could be too much.

• If custard is overheating, pour it quickly into cold bowl; whisk vigorously to prevent lumps forming.

• If custard has overheated, try dropping an ice cube into it, to rescue it from curdling.

• If cooked custard needs to cool before other ingredients are added to it, gently press dampened greaseproof paper on to surface of custard. Otherwise, a tough skin may form which will cause dessert to have a lumpy texture.

• A bain-marie helps custards bake evenly because it keeps the temperature constant and moderate, not too hot.

• To avoid spilling hot water when baking in a bain-marie, place filled ramekins or baking dish in large tin and centre tin on partially pulled out oven rack. Fill tin with hot water to come halfway up ramekins or dish, then gently push rack back into oven and bake custards as directed.

FRUIT AND NUTS

• An easy way to core apples and pears is with a melon baller. Just slice fruit in half and scoop out core in one smooth stroke.

• If using frozen raspberries to decorate top of dessert, take them from the freezer, spread them out on kitchen paper and thaw slowly in the refrigerator; they will retain their shape if used the moment they are thawed.

• When recipe calls for lemon or orange zest, that means thin yellow or orange outer layer of peel, not spongy white part (pith), which is bitter. Grate, using sharp grater, just before needed, because zest dries out quickly. Wash fruit before grating, and use unwaxed fruit if possible.

• To get maximum amount of juice when squeezing citrus fruits such as oranges, lemons or limes, gently roll fruit on work surface, pressing lightly, before halving and squeezing.

• If you have a microwave oven, use it to help squeeze citrus fruit juice more easily. Place fruit on oven floor and heat on High (100% power) just until fruit feels warm to the touch.

• Store all nuts (whole or shelled) in the freezer for maximum freshness. Wrapped in freezer bags, whole nuts will keep fresh for 3 years; shelled nuts for 1 year; ground nuts for 3 months.

• Whole nuts in their shells are much easier to crack when frozen because they are more brittle.

• Delicate torte or gâteau recipes often call for 'finely ground nuts' to replace some of the flour. For successful results, nuts must be ground very finely, yet be dry and light. Be careful not to process nuts in food processor or blender for too long; if they're thick and pasty, they will be too oily and heavy. If you are grinding the nuts by hand, grind two or three times to achieve correct texture. Packets of 'ground' nuts are not fine enough and must be ground again.

CHOCOLATE

Plain chocolate is made from basic cocoa solids, cocoa butter and other fats, cocoa powder and sugar. The more cocoa solids, the darker the chocolate; the more cocoa butter, the richer it will be. Bittersweet chocolate contains less sugar.

• *Milk* chocolate contains cocoa solids, cocoa butter and other fats, cocoa powder, sugar, milk and sometimes cream. Because of the relatively low amount of cocoa solids, milk chocolate cannot be substituted for plain or bittersweet chocolate.

• In recipes, use the best-quality plain dark chocolate you can find because it makes such a difference. Check the label before you buy, and choose the brand with the highest cocoa butter content. Most supermarkets and delicatessens stock good-quality plain chocolate; chocolat pâtissier is one of the best.

• *Plain chocolate flavour cake covering* is less expensive than real chocolate and does not have as fine a flavour. It contains less cocoa butter and more soft vegetable or nut fat. As a result, it is far easier to work with than real chocolate, especially when making chocolate decorations such as curls and caraque.

• *White* chocolate is really not chocolate at all, but a cooked-down mixture of fat, milk and sugar, with various flavourings added. Some white chocolate contains cocoa butter to give it a slight chocolate taste. White chocolate should only be used in recipes that specifically call for it.

• *Cocoa powder* is made from cocoa solids that have had nearly all cocoa butter removed. *Drinking chocolate powder* contains dried milk, sugar and flavourings; it should not be substituted for cocoa powder in recipes because it is too mild and sweet.

• You can substitute cocoa powder for chocolate as follows:
   For each 175 g/6 oz plain chocolate, use 6 tablespoons sifted cocoa powder plus 7 tablespoons caster sugar and 60 g/2 oz white vegetable fat or shortening.

• Store chocolate in cool, dry place. It keeps best if temperature is about 20°C/68°F, but not over 24°C/75°F.

• Chocolate stored in too cold conditions will 'sweat' when brought to room temperature.

• If chocolate is stored in too warm conditions, cocoa butter will start to melt and appear on surface of chocolate as a greyish-white coating. This does not affect flavour, and chocolate will return to its original colour when melted.

• Melting chocolate in the microwave oven: place 30 g/1 oz plain chocolate, broken into pieces, in small microwave-safe bowl. Heat on High (100% power) for 1-2 minutes, just until shiny (chocolate will still retain its shape). Remove bowl from the microwave and stir chocolate until melted and smooth.

• Melting chocolate in conventional ways: (1) Place in bowl over saucepan of gently simmering water. (2) Place in small dish or heatproof measuring jug and set in pan of hot water. (3) Place in heavy non-stick saucepan; melt over low heat – if pan is too thin, it will transfer heat too fast and burn chocolate. (4) For small amounts, leave chocolate in original foil wrapper; place on piece of foil and set in warm spot on cooker (not on burner).

• If chocolate does stiffen during melting, for each 90 g/3 oz of plain chocolate, start with 1 teaspoon and add up to 15 g/ ½ oz white vegetable fat (not vegetable oil, butter or margarine, which contain moisture), stirring until chocolate liquefies again and becomes smooth.

• Stir chocolate after it has begun to liquefy. If melting more than 450 g/ 1 lb, start with 225 g/8 oz and add remainder in 60 g/2 oz amounts.

• To speed melting, break chocolate into small pieces and stir frequently.

• When adding liquid to melted chocolate, always add at least 2 tablespoons at a time, to avoid chocolate stiffening.

• When making chocolate decorations, work with chocolate as soon as it is melted and smooth. When heated too long it can become grainy.

• To avoid breaking chocolate curls, pick them up with cocktail stick.

BAKING

• If recipe says to preheat oven, allow at least 10 minutes for it to reach baking temperature.

• Make sure tins are size called for in recipe and prepare them before you start.

• If cake tins are to be greased with melted butter or margarine, use pastry brush, or crumpled greaseproof paper or kitchen paper. ➤

• Grease fluted tins and moulds very generously, especially the ridges up the side and the central funnel, so cake can be turned out easily. The best way to do this is to brush tin or mould with melted butter or margarine, vegetable oil or shortening.

• If you do not have a springform cake tin, use a tin with a removable base – and vice versa.

• Place tins on oven rack so they do not touch one another, or sides of oven.

• Wait until minimum baking time given in recipe has elapsed before opening oven door; opening it too soon can lower oven temperature and make cake mixtures and doughs fall.

CAKES

• For 3 or 4 cake layers, 2 oven racks are needed, placed so oven is divided into thirds; stagger tins so one is not directly underneath another.

• To line a tin with non-stick baking parchment, place tin on paper and trace round base with tip of small knife. Cut out tracing and place in greased cake tin; it will fit exactly.

• For chocolate cakes, dust bottom and sides of tins with sifted cocoa powder rather than flour – it will not leave white film on cake.

• Be sure to follow timing guide given in each recipe for beating cake mixtures. If not beaten thoroughly, ingredients will not be evenly distributed and cake will fall; if overbeaten, cake may be tough and dry and will not rise properly.

• When beating cake mixture, scrape bowl often with rubber spatula for even mixing.

• When folding in, always fold light, fluffy ingredient into heavier one. Whisking part of beaten egg whites into heavy mixture lightens it and makes it easy to fold in remaining whites without reducing volume.

• For even textured cakes without any large holes, cut through mixture in cake tins with rubber spatula to remove any air bubbles, or gently tap cake tin on work surface just before baking.

• Cakes are done when they shrink away from side of tin and top springs back when pressed with finger.

• After removing cake from oven, leave to cool in tin on wire rack for about 10 minutes before turning out. If cake is cooled completely in tin, it may stick to bottom and side and be hard to remove; however, if cake is removed from tin while it is too hot, it could break.

• When baking powder is called for in a cake recipe, always add the exact amount specified. Do not be over-generous with baking powder as too much will cause cake to rise up beautifully in the oven and give you a false sense of security – cake will fall either just before it comes out of the oven or immediately after.

ICING AND FILLING

• For sandwich cakes, place first layer, top down, on plate; spread with filling, then place second layer, top up, on first, so flat bases of two layers face each other.

• Spread icing or firm filling to within 1 cm/½ inch of edge of cake, soft filling to 2.5 cm/1 inch of edge – weight of top layer will push it to edge.

• Spread cake with thin layer of icing first, to 'set' crumb, then ice again.

• When filling piping bag, stand narrow end in measuring jug or glass.

• To keep your piping bag sweet smelling, after each use, rinse it in warm water, then include it with a whites wash in the washing machine.

• A sturdy polythene bag makes a good piping bag. Fill, close with twist tie and snip small hole in corner.

FRUIT CAKES

• Line cake tin with foil to make cake easy to remove. Smooth out all creases, so side of cake will be smooth.

• Move oven rack to lower position to ensure whole cake is in middle of oven while baking.

• Mix dried fruit and nuts with a little flour before adding to mixture; this keeps them evenly suspended in mixture and prevents them from sinking to bottom while cake is baking.

• Spoon mixture evenly into tin and pack firmly to eliminate air pockets that will leave holes in baked cake.

• Test fruit cakes with a skewer or wooden cocktail stick inserted in centre; it should come out clean.

• Turn leftover fruit cake into an elegant dessert: slice cake into wine glasses, moisten with fruit juice or sherry and top with whipped cream.

PASTRY

• When making choux pastry dough, flour must be added as soon as liquid boils or water could evaporate and dough would not puff.

• Add flour for choux pastry dough all at once. Beat until smooth and formed into a ball that cleans side of saucepan.

• Pastries made with choux pastry dough should be eaten on the same day they are made, as pastry tends to soften quickly.

• Thaw frozen phyllo in its packet, otherwise it might dry out and crack.

• Once thawed, keep phyllo covered with damp cloth or cling film.

• Brush sheets of phyllo with melted butter – it adds flavour and keeps phyllo pliable so that it can be rolled or folded.

PIES

• What is the key to making good pastry? It is accurate measurement of ingredients, to ensure the correct balance of fat and flour, and not too much liquid. Too much flour makes tough pastry; too much fat results in a greasy, crumbly pastry. Too much liquid will require the excess flour that results in a tough crust.

• Roll out pastry dough on the coldest work surface possible – marble is ideal; granite and ceramic are also good.

• Roll out pastry as evenly as possible so edges are not too thin.

• When rolling out pastry dough, slide a pastry scraper or palette knife under it occasionally to make sure it is not sticking to the work surface. If it sticks, sprinkle work surface with more flour before continuing rolling.

• Never stretch pastry to fit into pie dish or tin; it will just shrink back when baking.

• After making a rope or fluted edge on a pie shell, hook points of pastry under rim of dish or tin so edge will stay in place as it bakes.

• For a shiny top, brush pastry with lightly beaten egg white. For a golden-brown glazed top, brush with beaten egg, egg yolk or milk.

• To help keep oven clean when baking fruit pie, place second oven rack below the one pie is on. Tear off sheet of foil, turn all edges up 1 cm/½ inch and place it on second rack to catch drips. Another way to catch drips from a fruit pie is to stand pie dish in a large roasting tin.

• To prevent soggy pastry in cream pies, try this: as soon as baked pie shell comes out of oven, brush it with lightly beaten egg white, making sure to cover areas pricked with fork. The heat from the hot pie shell will cook the egg white and form a protective seal to help eliminate sogginess after filling.

• If crumb crusts stick to pie dish or tin, set dish or tin on tea towel that has been wrung out in hot water and allow to stand briefly. It should then be easy to remove slices perfectly.

• After preparing your favourite pie, let your children use leftover pastry to make a special treat: get them to roll out dough and cut pretty shapes. While pie bakes, shapes can be browned in the oven at the same time, then spread with jam or sprinkled with cinnamon and sugar.

• When refrigerating a cream-topped pie, place it, uncovered, in a prominent position at the front of the refrigerator – this way everyone will notice it and it will not be knocked accidentally.

BISCUITS

• For a light texture, mix dough gently. Do not overwork dough or biscuits will be tough.

• No space to roll out biscuits? Shape dough into small balls, place 5-7.5 cm/2-3 inches apart on baking sheet and then press flat with bottom of a glass that has been dipped in caster sugar.

• Always start cutting at edge of dough and work towards centre, cutting biscuits as close together as possible to minimize scraps.

• Rehandling toughens biscuits, so press trimmings together – do not knead – before rolling again.

• Transfer fragile biscuits from board to baking sheet with fish slice to preserve shape.

• Always bake biscuits on heavy-duty baking sheets that do not bend or warp in the oven; silicone-coated baking sheets are now widely available, and are excellent for biscuit baking.

• Baking sheets should be at least 5 cm/2 inches smaller all round than your oven, so heat can circulate and biscuits can bake evenly.

• Always place dough on a cool baking sheet. It will spread too much on a hot one.

• Grease baking sheet only if recipe says so; very rich biscuits will spread too much if baked on greased sheets.

• After baking, transfer small biscuits at once from baking sheet to wire rack (they continue to bake on hot sheet).

• Cool biscuit bars completely in tin before turning out.

• Always cool biscuits completely before storing in airtight containers.

• When cutting up a tray of short-bread, cool to lukewarm, then mark into desired shapes and cut through; leave until almost cold before removing from tin. If you forget to mark and cut through, warm short-bread gently in oven again.

• Biscuits that are too hard can be softened by placing a slice of bread in the storage tin; change the slice every other day. A bread slice will also keep soft biscuits soft, just as it softens hardened brown sugar.

ICE CREAM AND FROZEN DESSERTS

• Ice cream, whether bought or home-made, keeps best in freezer at -18°C/0°F or lower.

• Ice cream will keep for 1 month in freezer compartment of refrigerator, or up to 2 months in home freezer.

• Do not re-freeze partially melted ice cream – a coarse, icy texture will result.

• To store open containers of ice cream, press cling film right on to exposed surface to protect ice cream from odours and prevent development of 'skin' or ice crystals.

• Partially frozen mixtures are ready for beating when firm 2.5 cm/1 inch round edge, though centre is still mushy.

Index

ACKNOWLEDGEMENTS

Editorial Director | Jeni Wright

Art Director | Denise Brown

Designers | Wendy Rogers
Sally Powell
Joanna Pocock

Editor | Nicky Vimpany

DTP Designer | Suzy Dittmar

Photography
Photographer's Assistant | All photography by David Murray
Jules Selmes

Home Economists
Step-by-steps and finished desserts
Finished desserts | Elizabeth Wolf-Cohen

Maxine Clark, Hilary Foster, Carole Handslip, Kathy Man, Janice Murfitt, Berit Vinegrad, Mandy Wagstaff

Stylist | Angi Lincoln

The companies listed here very graciously lent tableware | **Arthur Price of England** p. 68 (serving spoon); p. 69 (pie slice); p. 76 (forks); p. 81 (napkin rings); p. 85 (pie slice); p. 87 (sugar spoon); p. 90 (silver platter); p. 103 (forks)

Classical Creamware Limited p. 51 (plates, sugar bowl and shaker); p. 69 (plate)

Dartington Crystal p. 89 (glass bowl)

George Butler of Sheffield Limited p. 71 (pie slice); p. 79 (forks); p. 81 (pie slice and forks); p. 78 (forks); p. 89 (forks); p. 90 (pie slice); p. 93 (pie slice)

Josiah Wedgwood & Sons Limited p. 79 (plates); p. 93 (tray and plate)

Villeroy & Boch Tableware Limited p. 76 (glass plates); p. 195 (plate)

The publishers would also like to thank these companies for their assistance | Corning Limited
Neff U.K. Limited
Siemens Domestic Appliances Limited